MARKS THE SPOT

THEO HENDRIE

To everyone who has fallen between the cracks of society's view of gender – we see you. We accept you. You are home here.

Contents

5

Introduction

One of the hardest parts of being trans, for me at least, is how hard it can be to imagine the future. Especially before I came out, I found it so hard to think about where I might be in five years? Ten? Twenty? I simply couldn't picture life as a woman - because I'm not one.

Even now that I know who I am, there is so little representation for nonbinary people and even less for nonbinary people who aren't teenagers or twenty-somethings. Not only does this reinforce the idea that we're all just "young people trying to be special" but it makes it so hard to know what my life could look like as I grow older. When you grow up with not only no representation, but no image at all of a future you, it makes you feel like a ghost. How can you grow up, grow old, grow into yourself if there's no path for you?

Legally, we are ghosts too. In the UK, and most countries worldwide, there is no legal recognition for nonbinary people. Here there is no documentation to affirm our gender. We are not even asked about on the census, which prevents us from having any idea how many of us there are. And that in turn, prevents us getting access to the resources we so desperately need - how can we demand our rights when we don't even know how many people this impacts?

As a writer, I was very aware of all of this and of the importance of being able to tell our own stories. I knew that I wanted to help put that representation out there, to help carve one more place in the world for people like me. And so, this project was born.

I began with wanting to write on the nonbinary experience but what I quickly realised is that there is no singular nonbinary experience - and indeed, not everyone who is not a man or a woman, can be considered nonbinary. Rather than attempt to speak for everyone, I set about allowing them to speak for themselves and to find a way to use my platform to elevate the voices of others. In many ways, I am the stereotypical nonbinary person - blue-hair, androgynous, early twenties, and a bit of a social justice warrior. But there are as many ways to be nonbinary as there are people, just like there are many ways to be a man or a woman. I hope that X MARKS THE SPOT can begin to show the full diversity of our community.

It is thanks to our wonderful backers on Kickstarter that I was able to bring this project to life. As marginalized people, we don't have access to all the options that others do but crowdfunding and the help of all the wonderful people who shared it allowed us to level that playing field enough to bring the anthology to life. Our communities are so important for this reason, and I look forward to paying that forward as many times as I can.

Since one of the aims of the project is to show that we are not all the same, I can't ignore that we do not all agree on everything. This includes decisions as small as whether to spell it "nonbinary" or "non-binary" (which I have left according to how the author wrote it). Similarly, you will notice some disparity between British and American spellings throughout the anthology - I have made the choice to leave these as the author intended them, in order to keep it as close to their voice as possible.

Due to this, the choice of symbol on the cover was not an easy one to make. I wanted the anthology to have a symbol, to be instantly recognizable as something that discusses people outside the gender binary. One option was a mixture of the "man" and "woman" bathroom symbols. This was not ideal: it represents a cisnormative idea of being outside the binary and has an overreliance on gender stereotypes (men can, in fact, wear dresses). There is a nonbinary gender symbol, but it is far less known (defeating the purpose of the symbol in the first place). In the end, I opted for the symbol you'll see on the cover now - the transgender symbol - after putting it to an audience vote though this is not without its own flaws.

I hope that you will dip in and out of this anthology as you please. In its pages are many different stories and experiences. You may agree with some and not with others - that's okay. All I ask is that you make the effort to listen and to empathise. The world might be a better place if we could all do that.

"Dear Cis Person Who Picked This Up Looking For Answers"

This book is not intended to be for a cis gaze though I do hope that you can learn from it. I did not want the contributors to have to work overtime in order to explain themselves when this is their space to say what they want to say, so there is a glossary of terms at the end if you get confused.

Often when working to advocate for people outside the gender binary, we are asked to explain how or why our identities are a thing. You see, proving our existence is square one for nonbinary people whereas living our lives happily outside of the binary is square 99. While we understand that our existence is a new concept for many people - no one is born with this information after all - we cannot go back to square one every single time we are asked. If we did, we would

9

spend our entire lives having the same conversation over and over again instead of furthering our understanding of ourselves and our genders. For that reason, it was something I wanted to avoid wasting time with in these pages - all you really need to know is that we ARE a thing.

If that's isn't enough for you, however, consider this: for many nonbinary people, nonbinary is a transgender identity though not everyone labels themselves trans (see glossary for "transgender" and "non-cis" if this is confusing). If you know that it is possible for someone born with a vagina to be a man, and someone born with a penis to be a woman it should not be hard for you to understand that someone born with a vagina or a penis can be somewhere in between or something outside of man or woman. No one is quite sure what "causes" being trans though there are many theories. One is that it is due to hormones during foetal development. We know that hormones prompt sex development - as we all begin with the same body (hence why even cis men have nipples), these hormones stimulate us into developing genitalia and internal reproductive organs. It is now believed by some that this could also have something to do with our internal sense of gender.

Regardless of whether this turns out to be the case though, the important thing for you to understand is that we deserve respect whether or not you can find a reason for it. Our testimony should be reason enough - we know ourselves best.

There is no perfect language for us - right down to the fact that "nonbinary" describes what we're not rather than what we are. Not everyone who is outside the gender binary is nonbinary either as some come from cultures that never had the Western gender binary in the first place. I use nonbinary here because it is the term you have probably heard if you have heard of us at all.

If you have a friend or family member who is nonbinary and you are unsure what that means, please try to put aside what you think you know and just listen. Hear this from our own voices - from adults and teens alike - and try to understand. If someone has come out to you, it may seem sudden but know that they have probably been thinking about it for years before they told you. Try your best to understand them, to respect them. Ask them how you can help and be their biggest advocate. So much of the world is against us, don't add another voice to that.

If your child comes out as nonbinary, protect and love them fiercely. It doesn't matter if it might be a phase - that is how they feel, for however long they feel it. It might be a few months; it could be their whole life. And they will remember how you treat them now when they are most afraid. Be there for them, as best you can. It is okay to ask questions but be ready to listen - they may be your child but, on this at least, they know better than you. It's their life after all.

I hope that this book will go some way to telling you who and what we are.

"Dear Trans/Non-Cis/Questioning Person Who Picked This Up"

This one's for you.

No matter what labels you use, no matter if you're sure of your identity or not, no matter if you've been out for three months, twenty-years, since yesterday or not all. No matter if you're AMAB or AFAB or intersex, no matter how you present, this one's for you. I hope that this book will do you justice. I hope that you feel represented by its pages - I did my best to include as wide a range of our experiences as possible because we are of course, just as diverse and varied as any other group. But I hope it makes you feel seen, even if you cannot relate to everything.

If you are questioning, I hope that it provides some of the answers you seek. In the end, only you can choose your label, whatever that may be. I hope this goes some way to helping you find it even if nonbinary is not the label that you use for your whole life.

I know that much of the world is not built for us yet. I know that so many people are only just catching up to our existence. But we are making progress. I hope that this book can be one more tool for you to use to help teach cis people in your life and more than that, I hope that one day we won't need to teach those in our life anymore.

There may not be a path for us yet. But there are people, kind people, brave people who are surging ahead and paving that path to make the way a little easier for those behind them. I have to believe in those people. I have to believe there is a future - one that isn't binary.

Enjoy,
Theo

The Experiences

I Can be Anything

By Avi Burton (he/him & they/them)

It's a violent sort of
giving up
and a bloody requiem:
I can be anything, I
can be anything.

I built a marble shrine
to girl-me, body
pale and smooth and
curved, like paint
dripping down a wall.

Fig. 01 by Xanthe Wood (they/them)

I built a monolith to
boy-me, sharp
jutting into a new sky, like how
pride always comes before the fall.

It's a bitter sort of growing up
and still I am wrecked again.
I can be anything, I can be anything.

Fluid

By Nic Crosara (they/them)

I came out of the womb
creamy-pink but soon turned to brown
and naturally fell between the binary.
I had my mother's large teeth,
and my father's small mouth.
My body was graced
with the balance of both.
I left the haven of my throne
and went out amongst the masses.
I told them that I was a king,
a queen, a reckoning.
They gave me lash upon lash.
I have always found beauty in both
fantastical femininity
and magnetic masculinity.
Observers may assume
but I am not consumed
with assumptions and prejudice.
I am a king, queen, demon, wytch,
father, child, poet and muse.
none of the above, and yet all at once.
I look at my reflection and imagine
the construct of what it means
to be a part of humanity
and all I can identify with
is the freedom.

A Rose By Any Other Name

By Jaz Twersky (they/them)

Peter Amelia captivated me, and also didn't know who I was.

I was a 15-year-old self-proclaimed straight cis ally, at a conference with my high school's Gay Straight Alliance. Peter Amelia was another conference participant and the first nonbinary person I'd ever met. They wore tight jeans and a big knit poncho that had bright diagonal slashes of orange. They should have looked faintly ridiculous in that outfit, but instead, they looked incredibly cool, like they were living in the fashion of the future that I could never hope to approximate myself.

It was their name that stuck with me. Peter, as solid and mundanely male as the idiomatic Peter and Paul, matched with Amelia, a name that evoked the playful femininity of the *Amelia Bedelia* books I read as a child. Peter Amelia was not a name that would allow its bearer to slip seamlessly into the surrounding cis world; it demanded recognition. Peter Amelia wore their name's flamboyance as naturally as their vibrant poncho.

This encounter did not cause me to suddenly uncover my own queerness. I had to untangle that slowly, over the course of years, figuring out first my sexuality and then methodically making my way over to the knot of gender that I'm still picking my way through today. Sometimes, I think when I unravel it, there will be nothing there; there are, after all, practically infinite ways to tie a knot, but once you unravel it, it's all just string.

But before I take the thing apart, I want to know what to call it. I'm a writer; I've written poetry and prose, fiction and satire. I've tutored people in essay-writing, and I've edited news articles. I got a degree in linguistics. Which is all to say — I really, really, love words.

But I'm also the sort of person who's rarely found without yarn in my hands, so I know that there are many names for different kinds of knots. There are slips knots, reef knots, and diamond knots, as well as butterfly loops, Highwayman's hitches, and hangman's nooses, and that's not even mentioning the Windsor, the Prince Albert, or the four-in-hand. So much variety exists in the simple way that you can manipulate some string or cloth, and this variety is tremendously exciting to me.

Why isn't gender like that, for most people? Why can't they look at the profusion of possible options and marvel at how wondrous is all is? Why don't we have the same proliferation of words for it? Why is it that when, in college, I finally, tentatively, began to wonder if there was a reason I remembered Peter Amelia so vividly and had admired them so much, it wasn't possible for me to simply look up a list of genders, all generally agreed upon by a community of speakers?

My linguistics degree taught me that all living languages are capable of expressing all ideas native speakers want to express. The history of language suggests that we have, at any one point, enough words to describe our lived realities. When we don't have sufficient words, we create them.

Linguistics tells us that languages contain these things called "lexical gaps," which is when a language fails to have a word for something that the speakers want to talk about. It means there is an empty slot in our mental lexicon, a slot that can be filled if we can borrow or create a word to fill that gap. So if the name for our gender is a lexical gap, we can name it ourselves. If you look at a knot and say "what's that called?" and the world shrugs back and says it doesn't know, you are allowed to name it yourself.

The words for our genders fill lexical gaps. The neopronouns we use to refer to each other in the third person fill lexical gaps. The name Peter Amelia filled my own personal lexical gap.

I have begun to collect some of the words that fill in the gaps. I line them up like award-winning creations at craft shows, savoring the majesty of their mere existence: transgender, nonbinary, genderqueer, genderfluid, agender, genderflux, demigirl, demiboy, transmasc, transfemme, cisgender, gendervoid, bigender, polygender, tumtum, Māhū, juxera, proxvir, neutrois, androgynous, 'xie/xer', 'fae/faer'. Some of these words are ancient, and some I discovered last week. But this list, lovely as it is, still strikes me as threadbare.

One of the beautiful and frustrating things about being trans is that when we're presented with this knot that no one has named yet, we have the obligation and the privilege to name it ourselves.

And we do. We're damn good at it too. Who else picks their own names? Who gets a second chance like that, to pick a name based on who you are and who you want to be, as a full person facing the world in our own glory, to announce that our parents made a few mistakes when we were born and now we've come, leaping or ambling or hell, creeping cautiously on our hands and knees out of the closet to say hello, we're here now, and we'd like to introduce ourselves again.

Sometimes, there are common threads that seem to run through a group. Here are your Sams and your Katelyns, your Alexs and your Aidens. Here are your Elliots and your Emilys, your Chases and your

Chelseas. Someday, I want to see a massive study, right up there with the most popular baby names of the year, that tracks the most popular names among trans people from year to year, subdivided by age of transition. Do we mimic the most popular trends from the years we were born, or from the years we transition? Do we set the trends of names that will be popular a decade in the future? Are our names weirder, wilder, combinations of things that only we have? Has there ever been a cis person named Peter Amelia?

No one knows. Cis scientists don't study us, or at least fail to ask the interesting questions. I hope someday soon there will be more trans linguists, trans sociologists, trans biologists, trans historians, and trans people in every other discipline that involves describing the world around us. I hope there will be trans people in every profession, really, but there's something about being able to set the terms of discussion that feels revolutionary.

I once described myself as a "gender enthusiast." Naming myself thusly was an act of creation. It wasn't a knot. Knots are hard and self-contained. Knots begin things and end things; naming is neither a beginning or an end, but part of an ongoing process. It's like how in knitting, you start with a slip knot, but then you move on to a stitch, and from one stitch you go on to two, and from two you may proceed to a hundred thousand more stitches.

I have always liked being able to construct something that never existed before from a simple piece of string. Stitch one: I am nonbinary. Stitch two: I am transgender. Stitch three: my pronouns are they/them/theirs. Stitch four: My name is Jaz. Stitch five: I am a gender enthusiast who wishes to see the day our world fills with a hundred thousand genders. Stitch six: if we put our stitches together, perhaps we could knit a poncho out of gender, with big orange diagonal slashes, that would drape perfectly over any body, with any gender or lack thereof. I would give this poncho first prize and a place of honor in any craft show.

GENDER:???

Fig. 02 by Sidereus (they/them & xe/xyr)

SJW Vocabulary

By Marius Thienenkamp (he/him & they/them)
Content warnings: *transphobia, family issues, gaslighting*

There exists a generally observed phenomenon where the more you know or experience about any given topic, the less you can evaluate how much the general public knows about it. Similarly, one of the most frustrating and emotionally taxing aspects of being neither a man nor a woman is realizing that the general public, on a fundamental level, will not be able to understand you.

I learned this the hard way when I came out to my family as genderqueer/non-binary in the summer of 2017. I had chosen a family dinner at one of our favorite restaurants shortly before my parents would leave for vacation and I would move out of their apartment. I stuttered all the way through. Instead of the validation and reassurance I had expected from my considerably liberal family, what I got as a response was mostly confusion. "Why can't you just be an atypical boy? Why would you need to express that? You need to give us time to deal with this."

On top of that, my family was concerned about the discrimination I would face – an admirable motif. But still ultimately harmful if it means wanting me back in the closet and therefore contributing to the very same discrimination. I know it's unfair to expect my family to completely understand what this new identity of mine would entail in the way that I myself do. And I never did. Still, some hurtful things were said afterwards that are not easy to forget – my mother insisting that she still sees me as a man and that I "would have to be one due to male genitalia" comes to mind.

The difference between coming out as non-binary and coming out as gay is that virtually everyone knows what being gay means. This is not to say that coming out as gay should be regarded as harmless, and I am in no position to claim that. It changes nothing about the vile homophobia and actual safety risks that still exist in far too many families. Though in the specific case of my parents and grandma, it would have helped had they even had a concept of what it was that I was coming out to them as.

Social media bubbles have been criticized to the moon and back, and I'm not interested in completely dismissing them and their potential to provide safe spaces for expressing senses of self. At the same time, we often rely on mutual validation and affirmative "SJW ("Social Justice Warrior") vocabulary" to such a great extent that we lose our perspective on how we can effectively communicate with people outside of the bubble. My point is not that validation and accurate vocabulary aren't vital. My point is that I had almost forgotten how everyday cis people like my family think and talk about trans issues until I was personally confronted by it.

I recently found a collection of journals I did as a writing exercise around the time of coming out. Re-reading them reminded me of something: the most ironic aspect of how coming out turned out for me was that I had previously been convinced that none of it would be that big of a deal. So, what if I don't really see myself as a man anymore? But the concept seemed to be so incredibly foreign to my family that is must have genuinely felt like losing the ground below their feet.

And we haven't even gotten to coming out to people who aren't close family yet. In my case, many of

my friends found out after reading the first article I ever wrote on the subject. I felt
awkward coming out to them individually, and I think the fear that their reaction might be disappointing is not completely unwarranted. As a non-binary person, there will often be no shortage of friends who downplay or discount your needs.

Some will be weirded out by your coming out to them and just not talk about it anymore. Some will generally be supportive but still, misunderstand the concept. And a lot of them will misgender you, even if not always deliberately. I don't want to downplay the overwhelming amount of people who have been supportive and affirmative. But even they can't fully understand what I am going through – although this is not their fault.

And then there's a huge amount of people who you're not even sure if it's worth coming out to. Random people at uni. Random people at work. Random family members that you rarely see. Sure, you want to live as your authentic self. But is it really worth the emotions of explaining the whole concept to them? My personal answer to this question has always been "no" – because I had no idea how to approach that situation.

There is a common stereotype that non-binary people are attention-seeking brats who just can't stop talking about their genders and pronouns and safe spaces. Firstly, I think that in a world where downright absurd masculinity rituals make up a significant portion of almost every cis man's life cycle, I don't see why non-binary people shouldn't also be allowed to talk about their genders But secondly, the stereotype is dangerously untrue for a lot of us.

Being afraid to weird others out or thinking that they wouldn't understand anyway are real fears for nonbinary people that often keep us from speaking up or expressing ourselves. I sure know that this has been the case for me. This has put me in a weird spot where I see myself as a person who would love to celebrate pride but is terrified of even saying the label that describes my gender out loud. I have a genderqueer pride flag hanging in my bedroom, but I'm scared shitless of telling others what it means.

Over the course of my first year of living as genderqueer more or less openly, this sense of isolation and feeling misunderstood culminated in a lot of behaviour that I now realize was not entirely fair to myself. This included seeking out "There are only 2 genders!!!!" type videos on YouTube and getting increasingly frustrated – and frightened. What I seemed to be up against was a pop cultural wave of pushback against a group I belong to. So, I gaslit myself: "What if I'm making this all up because I think too much about it? What if I need to question myself more when it comes to who I am?".

Make no mistake: this sentiment was really toxic. Taken together with the disappointment from minor but invalidating experiences with friends and the ongoing misgendering from my parents and grandma, a bigger picture started to form: "I'm not sure people understand me or are on my side on this". I decided that isolating myself with these thoughts would only make things worse. And I knew that knowing I could count on the people that mean most to me would give me strength again. One year after my coming-out I decided to have another in-depth talk with my family about my gender.

This conversation went a lot better. I was able to get to the root of the problem when my dad decidedly claimed that I "couldn't expect anyone" not to call me a man or boy. Exploring the issue further I realized that my family knew virtually nothing about the effects of misgendering and the centrality of having one's identity recognized for trans people. Again, I had completely overestimated what the average person knows about trans issues because I had lost that perspective. But at least now I knew what one of the cruxes of the problem in communication we were facing was. I understand that it took a privileged position for me to be able to have this talk with my family and that this sort of discussion is not safe or recommendable to everyone. But, I thought, at least in my case, things could get better.

And they did get better for a while. Then they got worse again. I don't know if my parents and grandma will ever quite "get" my gender identity in the way that I would wish they did. While the thought that they will only ever see me as a man with nail polish is scary, it's also not really that far-fetched. The reason I can't just ignore this is that I feel a central part of who I am is being disregarded. This and the fact that being called a boy or a man causes me actual discomfort.

If there's a lesson I took from the last two years, it's this: in order to make coming-outs and the lives we lead after them safer and less emotionally draining for non-binary people, we need to create awareness for our identities and needs in mainstream society. The feeling of isolation and being misunderstood I have experienced in regard to my gender in the last few years seems to fundamentally stem from the lack of this awareness. Especially in otherwise fantastic people – because make no mistake, I love my parents and grandma with all my heart. Finding out how we and our allies can effectively communicate with those unfamiliar with the genders beyond man and woman is perhaps one of the greatest current challenges for the LGBTQ+ community.

Doorways

By Theo Hendrie (he/him & they/them)

At first, you try to blend in.
A simple uniform, jeans and a t-shirt,
never talk too loud, never smile too bright,
don't stare too long in case
they guess you want to be them,
resist the urge to wander
to the other side of the store
and fill your arms with clothes
that are for people who are not you.

Cringe at the sign over the bathroom door
you must walk through but know
that the other door isn't for you either.
You are a jigsaw piece that just won't fit
into this last tight gap. Begin to wonder

if there will ever be a door you can step
through without leaving part of yourself outside.

Later, when the cloak from the closet
gets too stifling, cast it off.
Go overboard. Decorate your walls
with rainbow tapestries, paint glitter
on your cheeks like war paint,
walk the streets with the flashing
arrow of your dyed hair marking you out.

Different. Other. Queer.

Collect pin badges and crowd them
together on your jacket so they

are the first thing anyone sees when
they look at you. Pronoun pins and
"attraction beyond gender" and
rainbows and clenched fists raised proud.
Better they are bombarded by
your personal propaganda
than they judge you when
they can't categorise you neatly enough.

Eventually, you will grow so used
to this new suit of armour that
it won't feel tight anymore.
When you feel them staring, tell yourself
it's just that you have your brightness turned
all the way up, not that they're judging.
If you have to be stared at,
make it happen on your terms.

Eventually, you will know every safe spot in town.
And you will smile to walk through the doors,
with all of you intact.

Fig. 03 by Maddy Test (they/them)

28

How I Didn't Know I Was Trans

By Elliot Walsh (he/him)
Content warnings: *internalised transphobia*

I think I've watched every "How I Knew I Was Trans" and "How To Know If You're Trans" YouTube video in existence. A common theme throughout these videos is "I feel like I've known for my whole life," or "I've always known something was different about me" or "I always liked [insert stereotypically gender-specific interests here] only," etc. Of course, this isn't always the case, but it seemed like almost every video I watched had some iteration of this. Which kind of sucked, if I'm being honest. I mean, great for them. But not so great for a very confused and distraught me. Because I, like many other trans kids, didn't have that experience.

I didn't know I was trans. I had no idea. No signs. No clues. No funny feeling. I just didn't know. Until, suddenly, I did. And even when I knew, I wasn't sure. I wasn't sure of the words, of how to say I was close to the binary but that there's a little something different that places me outside of it. I didn't know how to explain that something in words or feelings, either to myself or to others.

So, whether it was to validate myself, or to fit in, to try and find a definitive "reason" for being trans, or a mixture of the three, I struggled to squeeze myself into that box of people who had known since they were kids or teenagers. Inside that little box, I tried to further squeeze myself into another smaller box of binary stereotypes like some sort of transgender Russian nesting doll.

I came up with the brilliant idea of making a list. I would look into my past for the "common signs" of being

29

trans as kid. So, I could say "DUH! Of course, I knew all along!" I forced myself to think as I struggled to come up with the 'clues' from my childhood. Making a methodical, finite list of traits and qualities, likes and dislikes, seemed easier to me than that only I could tell myself my gender. At the time, that thought was fucking terrifying.

So, I made a list instead. But even that list was bound to the assumptions of the gender binary or "binary box rules" as I like to call them. It looked something like this:

1. I never liked dresses. In order to convince me to wear one to a family event, my dad once told me that wearing a dress was the only way I would be comfortable during the car ride. I cried, but I did it. I told him I wanted to wear a tuxedo for my wedding. He said only boys could do that. I was upset, but not life-changing upset, you know?
2. I only wanted to play baseball, not softball. Baseball always seemed cooler to me because that's what the Red Sox played. In the end, I was forced to join softball when I was ten. I loved it.
3. I cried one year on Christmas because my Nana gave me bras in front of everyone. I'm still salty about this.
4. I insisted I only liked "boy" colors like green and blue in preschool. A boy told me I could only like pink and purple, which is why he had stolen my green marker. I told him he was being a butthead. I got put in time-out.
5. I had mostly guy friends (until someone made fun of me and my best friend for having "guy-girl sleepovers." Then I didn't have any guy friends).

6. I was upset when I got my first period. But maybe that was because I thought I was going to bleed out and die.
7. I didn't like "girl" toys. I got given a Bratz doll for Christmas one year. My friend and I spent the next few weeks putting it in my driveway and laughing when it would get run over by my neighbor's truck.

I triumphantly stared at my list (seven whole signs!) for a good minute. All of the things on this list did happen and are true. But it doesn't mean jack-shit about my transness.

So, what if I didn't like dresses? Do you know who else doesn't like dresses? A fuckton of people of all genders. So, what if I cried when I got bras for Christmas in front of my family? What nine-year-old wouldn't get super embarrassed opening underwear in front of their Uncle and his nice, but overbearing, girlfriend? So, what if I was upset when I got my period? Periods aren't fun for anyone. So, what if I had mostly guy friends? So, what if I only like blue as a five-year-old? My cis friend Jessie's favorite color was blue as well. Does that make her trans? And what about people who had those multi-colored markers? What gender does that make them, by my own list-logic? Your gender isn't decided by the things you like or the clothes you wear.

I stared at my list for a little while longer as I methodically refuted each and every clue I had thought of. Each 'sign' from my childhood crumbled away until I was simply grasping at straws. At that point, I think might've cried in the library (not an uncommon occurrence during college if I'm honest). I crumpled up the list and recycled it. (I know it would've been cooler and more dramatic if I'd thrown the list into the garbage, but climate change is a real fucker, you know?).

I didn't know I was trans. Until I did. And even that came with some ambiguity since I knew I wasn't binary. Gender is something no single list, word, or experience can fully articulate. On some level, I wish it were that easy. That way I could've saved myself a lot of angst and a lot of spent watching "How To Know If

Fig. 04 IridescentScales (they/them)

You're Trans" videos on YouTube (which would give me literally days of my life back).

Sometimes I had even wished I was a binary trans person as though that would make it easier. But no trans experience is easy. My struggles to understand my gender can't compare to anyone else's because my experience is uniquely my own, uniquely tough, uniquely enigmatic. There's no list to check off. There's no experience you have to have. There aren't any prerequisites to being trans. Even if you don't know like other people knew. Even if your non-binary is different from someone else's non-binary. Even if you don't know when other people know. Even if you never fully know. Even if there are no words or lists to explain how you simply are.

There's just what you know, even if you're not 100% sure. You get to decide.

Coming Out In The Most Magical Place On Earth

By Mika Holbrook (he/him & ze/zir)
Content warnings: *misgendering, transphobia*

I am genderfluid. For years now I have tried to be upfront about it, to curb the "ma'ams" and "shes" before they start to sting. In college, it's simple: an email to professors and a pronoun button for students. Then, I got a job at Disney - known for being notoriously strict about employee appearance and conformity, which the very nature of my gender defied.

Fig. 05 by Mel G. Cabral (they/them)

I mentioned I was trans in my phone interview and was reassured that it wouldn't be an issue. I was part of the Disney College Program, at the recommendation of a friend (also trans) who had done it before. I interrogated them about their experience, from housing to fellow cast members and managers. I studied up on everything Disney's career website had to offer, particularly Disney Look, a dress code that rivalled Catholic schools in its severity and adherence to gender roles. Though not yet employed, I acted as a model cast member. I shaved my pink undercut and tried to shape myself into the image of a presentable cis man.

When August of 2016 rolled in, I traded dry California nosebleeds for Orlando humidity filling my lungs. 'Casting,' where jobs were assigned and fingerprints were scanned, went smoothly enough until at the Disney Look check, I asked how I should handle my uniform, my 'costume,' when I started at my location. "I'm genderfluid, you see," I started, "So will I be able to switch costumes if they're gendered? Will I have to just pick one?" The cheery smile on the cast member's face slipped into blank confusion before she pulled me aside, out of the way of those just trying to get confirmation that their haircut was right, and their tattoos were covered.

"I'll go ask someone," she said and slipped away while I sat, watching others pass through, their eyes looking over me with confusion. An hour and a phone call with Disney's Pride team later, there were no real answers, just an offer to switch me to a position with gender-neutral costumes which I quickly shot down when I heard my current role let me wear suspenders.

When I finally started my on-site training, "earning my ears" as a merchandise cast member on Sunset Boulevard in Hollywood Studios, I was met with the same confusion from my trainers when I eyed the suspenders rather than the skirts. They looked at each other, frowning, before asking me to wait while they consulted someone else. An older man in a sunhat and a name badge with several pins declaring his seniority helped me find each piece of the costume in the proper size. While he taught me how to tie the tie that completed the look, he spoke.

"Just wear this," he said, straightening it against my collar, "so your managers won't get confused."

With the costumes so heavily gendered, based on clothes worn by Walt Disney himself and his wife to suit our faux-40s Hollywood setting, I'd expected that even if my voice was too high, my co-workers would err on the side of caution and call me "he," or at least ask for my pronouns quietly as one of the other trainees did during our first lunch break together. Yet just after that break, as I was being led around a store styled like the Carthay Circle Theater, a woman in the dotted red outfit colloquially known as the "strawberry" costume exclaimed, "I didn't know we could wear the men's costume!" That "we," the implied relationship in a single syllable, crushed me.

My trainers, though they had witnessed the painful process of choosing a costume, didn't pick up on the reason, even when I had used the word "genderfluid" to explain my decision. I was lumped in with the three women training with me and set apart from Mike, the only one at that point who'd taken care to not misgender me. Over the next few weeks, only two others asked: a trainer who was rarely in the area but knew nonbinary people and wanted to correctly gender me on the occasions we saw each other and one of the coordinators, who knew me already from the LGBT College Program Facebook. To everyone else, my costume was just a quirk, something I got away with because of my short hair. Really, they knew or thought they knew, I was a girl. I was alone in a world that barely felt real, constantly referred to as though it was a never-ending play or movie set. I did not know how to correct them, though every day I tried to deepen my voice and kept my chest bound, hoping they would notice and take a hint.

Even under the best circumstances, the college program is brutal. When the holidays rolled in, our hours climbed from the minimum 33 to 50+, every single week. Sunset was hit particularly hard, as a popular and severely understaffed area. We drank to cope, iced our feet for the pain, downed Dayquil like candy in order to stay standing. We maintained immaculate rows of plush dolls and plastered smiles on our faces while stressed holiday-goers screamed in our faces about events beyond our control. August to January, I bore this alongside every "she," every "ladies," every "miss." Alongside the whispers from co-workers who called me a freak because they knew my gender but couldn't accept it. After my entire pay check for the week of Christmas and New Years' went to a doctor's visit and a bottle of vodka, I broke. Turning to the world (Facebook) for advice, for anything, I asked, "How do I tell them I am not what they think I am?"

From friends, I received words of comfort and anger on my behalf. "How could they not know?" The coordinator, now gone, was furious - every chance she'd had, she'd defended me, corrected others, and still, the misgendering persisted. Mike, who had known since the beginning, messaged me as well.

"If you want to tell a manager, talk to Sal," the one who was widely known as the kindest, who let us sample candy and caramel apples from Sweet Spells when he closed, "cause I'm pretty sure he's gay."

I agonized over 'coming out' for a solid week. I had legitimate fears, as a cast member without the protection of a union, who could be fired on the spot and sent home without any real reason if somebody decided to take issue with my identity. I also had other, stupid anxieties. What if they think I'm faking? What if this is oversharing? What if they just stare blankly, confused, no longer seeing me as a human but as the freak that others called me? I was Shakespearean in my melancholy, sprawling across tables during my lunch breaks in despair. It took until the closing rush, just before I was meant to clock out, to ask Sal to talk.

We ducked out of the store, through the stockroom and to 'backstage,' the alleys between the buildings where cast members, whether they were characters or not, could take their masks off. Amid lockers, dumpsters, and vending machines, in the fading haze from the fireworks, I forced myself to speak.

"I should've said this when I started, but, I'm trans." I had one hand tugging at my rolled-up sleeve, nearly tearing the fabric in its intensity. My eyes fixated on the ground, not daring to look at Sal's face. I explained genderfluidity - how sometimes I was more a man, sometimes more agender, only rarely the woman that people assumed I was - and told him my pronouns. When I was done, I finally looked and saw none of the expressions I had feared. At worst, he was concerned, and when he spoke, he reassured me and thanked me.

"I know this can be hard, it was difficult for me to come out to my family," he said, and I nearly cried. I let go of my sleeve and relaxed, bit by bit. The worst was over, and I knew there was someone, at least one person, in management who was on my side. Sal asked if he could hug me and I accepted, squeezing tightly.

The work didn't get easier, but I felt lighter, and as the weeks passed by the misgendering lessened, at least from Disney itself. Guests were entities beyond anyone's control, and I made peace with that. When the end of my program came in May, I stopped by Hollywood Studios at opening time and found my way to the shops I'd worked for nearly a year in order to see Sal.

"I just wanted to say thank you, and goodbye," I said, cringing at myself and my word choice, but I couldn't find any other words for what the program and his support had meant. And Sal smiled and said the sappiest possible response: "You'll always have a home on Sunset."

Presenting While Nonbinary
By Donnie Martino (he/him)

My life has improved tremendously since I started identifying as non-binary. It was a long time coming. As someone who came of age on LiveJournal, the resources for non-binary identities for me were pretty slim. The term 'genderqueer' was beginning to be thrown around, but it was a nebulous phrase that I identified with because I knew I wasn't really cis and I also knew I wasn't a man. I hung onto it for years until I was able to find out about non-binary identities through other social media platforms, specifically 2009-2012 era Tumblr. Specific labels changed here and there, but some time toward my senior year of college, I landed on agender and have stuck with it ever since.

The thing about non-binary identities is that while they help you put your gender, or lack of it, into words, they don't really give you much guidance on presentation. By no means does this mean that they should. If being non-binary has taught me one thing, it's that societal expectations are not exactly put into place to help us feel good about our bodies. But there is something daunting about deciding that you don't have a gender, even when your body gets mercilessly gendered by anybody and everybody. Being agender makes sense for me and I've been able to explain it to my trans friends with ease. I've even been able to explain it to the cis people I keep close with a decent success rate. But whenever I've left this inner circle, I've struggled with even allowing myself to say anything about it.

It doesn't help that my outer circle has some high stakes. In my case, it has to do with my professional identity. I have worked with children for as long as I could legally work. Since then, my responsibilities have ranged from being a camp counselor, to a classroom teacher, to an assistant camp director, to now being a director of student affairs at an after-school program. Each one has put me in a position where I've had to decide if I felt comfortable disclosing my gender and sexuality to my bosses. So far, I've been able to be out about my sexuality, but the gender aspect has always tripped me up a bit. I used to assume that all of this had to do with my fear of having parents question my ability to take care of children because they saw my identity as some sort of deviance. It's been a legitimate fear at some of the schools I've worked at, even if it's not as big a fear at my current job. But I think that a lot of it nowadays is just that I don't have the emotional energy to explain how my gender identity works in relation to how I present.

I can't speak for everyone, but my presentation as a non-binary person has featured many different fluctuations. I'm sure anyone would agree that people should just focus on doing what is good and safe for them in terms of presentation. But I think it's important to be prepared for the good and safe aspect to change dramatically, sometimes hour-to-hour. Sure, some of this is circumstantial. For example, the clothes I wear in work are a lot of chunky sweaters and loose flannels. They're clothes I can chase middle schoolers in, with the unintended benefit of being able to be categorized as "probably performs an alternative lifestyle." I wear a lot of these clothes outside of work, as well. As I write this, I've been in a bit of a masculine-presenting moment, usually wearing the more casual versions of those articles of clothing in my wardrobe. But there are spikes of feminine-presentation that I enjoy, though it's usually

41

constrained to that inner circle of queer and trans people I'm involved in. For example, that group is probably the only people who have seen me wear earrings in years. When I travel, I have to pack way more clothes than I intend to wear, because I just don't know when I'm going to feel good and safe, nor do I know when gender dysphoria is going to render certain outfits unwearable. My luggage is always full of low-scooped tops for when I don't mind my chest exposed, button-ups when I definitely don't want it to be, grey-tinted lipstick if I want to look slightly alien, and green lipsticks when I want to look unmistakably so. It's a bit of a nightmare to prepare for, especially when I'm going on long trips, but it's been the way to keep me from ending up in a situation where nothing worked for me.

It's a hard thing to talk about with people, even if it makes so much sense in my head. It's another success and struggle of being non-binary. It's such a personalized experience because it should be. It's your gender, combination of genders, or lack thereof. But it also means that whatever you're experiencing is purely your own, and you're not always going to get the camaraderie you might be looking for. I'm glad that I am surrounded by people that have been able to look at these aspects of my presentation and have not questioned it. In fact, I am eternally grateful for it.

This lack of structure is probably why I get so hung up on coming out at work. I've been able to do little things. For example, my deadname no longer exists on any aspect of my organization's website and records, outside of my legal documents. It's legitimately amazing how seriously people take your name when it's your display name on your email account. Also, I use 'she/her' pronouns at work, but I never actually call myself a woman or respond to being labeled as such.

It's almost a game for me at this point, especially when working with kids. Once I was meeting a colleague's twin girls and one of them took a look at my short hair and snapped, "Are you a boy?" I just grinned and asked, "And what if I was?" trying not to laugh as her face screwed up in frustration.

I hope that someday I will feel comfortable enough to come out as non-binary at work. This may just have to do with my confidence in my position, along with some little presentation details. For example, I'm currently saving up for top surgery. I don't see it as a magical solution. I don't think there ever really is when you're agender, at least in the way that gender presents itself in society. But it might be what I need to just start asking for the correct pronouns. But if it isn't, I won't let myself become upset about it. I am trying to disrupt presentation in my own ways, on my terms. It's allowed me to be able to work with hundreds of students and support them academically and emotionally. While it may not have always been overt, I hope that a few of them felt a little more comfortable with their own gender presentation, even if it was only for a class or two.

Ultimately, presentation, when you are non-binary, is a journey. It may be a short one for some people, but for a lot of people, it's going to be a long one, perhaps for the rest of their lives. But I don't think it has to be a scary one. You will find what works for you, you'll find what doesn't. It doesn't have to be scary, but definitely make sure you pack for any potential outfit changes along the way.

A Collection Of Unfinished Statements

First published by *VIDA Review*
By RBrown (they/them)

Content warnings: *body dysmorphia, misgendering, bathroom harassment, mental illness*

I felt sexy for the first time in a long time when I first wore a binder, like my body was finally something that belonged to me.

I don't hate my body. This is something that I tell myself and sometimes believe. It feels true and not true.

A friend of mine was running a speculative fiction contest once and I submitted a speculative fiction poem. "This is a poem," she said. "But it's speculative," I said or thought. This is how I feel most of the time, trying to fit my body in spaces where I don't always feel like I belong.

Sometimes I have to remind myself that the friends who I've made through writing are some of the people who care about me the most, who make the greatest effort to use my correct pronouns and try to include me in conversations, to remember that there are people like me who exist outside of the binary.

Sometimes I feel like I am outside of everything.

I hate being the trans friend, feeling like I am something that will never fit.

I love my friends.

Most of the time I feel like my body is something separate from myself. This is an explanation and it is not.

Sometimes I cry thinking about the people I love using the right pronouns for me.

The first time I felt like I fit in my body was when I changed my pronouns. That's the only way I know how to say it.

I spent my whole life up to that point feeling like I didn't fit inside my body and I didn't know why, and then suddenly I did.

Lately, everything I write turns into an apology, or a list of things that I'm afraid of, which, I think, is another kind of apology.

I am afraid for my body. For what it represents to people who don't know me, who don't understand.

I've been harassed for using the wrong bathroom. Now I'm afraid of that too.

There are things that I want to explain to my friends and one of these things is the fragility of the place that me and people like me occupy in society. If being harassed for using the bathroom is the worst thing that ever happens to me, it's nothing. This is not the worst thing that could happen to my body.

I want to explain to my friends the look you get when someone is afraid of you. When someone doesn't know what box to put you in. I want to explain that there is a way that I see this same look in the pause before someone says my name. The look in someone's eyes as they are trying to say the right things around me.

The thing about coming out is that it never stops. Every time I meet a new person, I have to start all over again. I have to explain myself. I have to explain why it's okay for me to be this way. I feel like I take up too much space. I feel like I am asking for so much for other people just to see me. To exist.

Sometimes I want so desperately to have a "normal" life. Sometimes I feel like this is too much to ask for, like I'm not a good queer person because I'm not always fighting. Sometimes I am very, very tired.

I work very hard to appear non-threatening in public, like if I can be just a little nicer, just a little kinder, just a little softer, just a little smaller, then maybe no one will notice me. Maybe I will blend in. Maybe today will be another day where I get by without anyone hurting me.

Mostly when people ask me how I identify I say, I don't. For other trans people, this is usually enough. For others, this is more difficult. "But what *are* you?" they seem to be asking "What box can I put you in?"

Days, where I am inside my body, are good days. Days, when I am outside my body, are just days, sometimes bad days.

Sometimes I wake up after disassociating for a week or more at a time and I see the whole world again. I feel things in a way that I think I am supposed to feel them.

It is impossible for me to talk about my trans self without talking about mental illness. For me, it is hard to pull apart the two. I had a therapist once, or more than once, who tried to say that the two were connected. That one made way for the other. I learned to put aside that kind of binary thinking a long time ago. Both/and? One or the other? I am afraid and I am afraid for my safety.

It is a weekday night in Tuscaloosa, Alabama, where I go to school and teach and write and I am anxious. I am wearing my binder and a new button-up shirt. I look good, but I am still afraid.

Later, I will go to a party full of people who I love and I will spend the whole night adjusting my shirt and pulling at my hair, ticks that I do more when I am nervous, but, quite frankly, find myself doing most of the day. My friend's house has big ceilings that I find constricting when the room is full of people, which tonight it is. I am misgendered at least four times, I think, by people who don't know me, or who do, and would feel sorry if they knew what they were doing.

I don't know how to stop this. How to correct someone. It is a kindness that I am still trying to learn how to give myself.

This is not what I want to say though. What I want to say is this, that night before the party, I go to the grocery store and I am afraid. I am afraid that today is the day that someone will decide that I so obviously don't belong here. That my body is not the right body. I feel like I can be seen by everyone in town. At the checkout, the clerk says, "I like your shirt!" and I am flooded with relief. I am brought back to myself. For a moment, I am safe.

I want to tell my friends about what it feels like to be inside and outside of my body, sometimes at the same time. I want to explain how it feels to be afraid of everyone that you see. The fear of other people's fear. The fear that I will always be on the outside. The knowledge of what happens to people like me.

Maybe this is how I will start.

Learning Curve

By Ronnie Vlasáků (they/them)
Content warnings: *misgendering*

How do I say this?
It's not much to ask for.
I've even told you before
but you seem to forget every time.
I guess it's easy to miss
If your ears aren't tuned to the chime.

Maybe you should pay attention
to the words you say.
Is it that hard to use 'they'?
Just one of those things I won't mention.
How do I avoid guilt for speaking up?
Hurting me might not be your intention
but it's the third time just today
I'm tired of excusing you in my head.
Some names should just stay dead.

You never remember
what you've already known.
It's like we're a team working in tandem
and then suddenly I'm stranded
It makes me feel so alone
It's different when it's a stranger
I can shrug it off if they say 'her'
but this is another thing
and it stings.

But it's only the adjustment period, right?
It just takes time to get used to.
There's progress I'm not seeing.

Should I even bother correcting you?
It feels like a useless fight
like something I gotta tolerate
for the time being.

Checkmark

By Castor Santee (they/them)
Content warnings: *misgendering*

Sometimes I sit down and list all the checkboxes that fall under my understanding of "identity." Black, lesbian, nonbinary, femme, pagan, mentally ill and a hundred more. To look at all of them together can be overwhelming and in an age of Facebook comment sections and MAGA hats, it seems the more intersectional your existence is, the less respect you receive. The more different from the established norm you are, the more you're a "snowflake" and although I have a full understanding that this opinion should not affect me, it does. The idea that one can read all the horrible things that should happen to you simply because your life has been dealt different cards and feel absolutely nothing is a scam. We notice how our shoulders droop when we recognize that difference, especially as children.

I'd always known I had more boxes checked than everyone else in my tragic little Texas hometown. There was never a moment in my life that I considered myself straight, but upon leaving that tragic town and coming to college in a state where snow isn't an occasion for community-wide panic, things got complicated.

All it took was one class with one friend who used the pronouns "they/them" and it was as if everything clicked together, but not necessarily in the best way. I was on a sort of hero's journey of understanding who I was, and this was the moment of resistance. I hated how curious I was about this. I hated how I couldn't stop thinking about how liberating it would be to exist outside of a pre-established binary and I hated that I now had the choice to do so.

I firmly believe that there are people who put off finding that journey their entire lives and it is a choice to do so. The choice is easier for some, like my parents, who didn't know there were ever more letters than LGBT, but the blindfold had been ripped off my face and now I had to confront the fact that everything my friend was telling me about their experience eerily mirrored mine.

Just as there was never a point in my life where I considered myself straight, there was never really a point where I considered myself a girl. The phrase "young lady" made my skin crawl, but I could never fully put my finger on why. I was considered a tomboy right up until tomboy became adjacent with "lesbian" and the push to become a respectable young woman started. It all felt incorrect. Nothing about being a strong, independent woman felt empowering or liberating to me. It wasn't until I finally asked this friend that introduced me to nonbinary genders if there was a word for not identifying with any binary gender at all.

They responded with the word "agenda" (agender) and I never looked back.

The social transitions have been hard. It took me months to get the courage to tell people to refer to me with the singular "they" and it took years for me to tell people to call me by my new name. I still feel like a burden when they have to correct themselves. Not because they aren't accepting, but people with enough check marks under their identity know the tension in the room when someone thinks you're a freak but is too scared to tell you that to your face.

My sudden coming of age moment was hit with a wall of frustration when I remembered that I'm a lesbian and that word is as important to me as the color of my skin. Being black, femme and a dyke was vital to who I am as a person and the concept of gender took all that and stuck it in a blender. My love for women was rooted in me being a woman as well, I thought, and now that I realized I wasn't, what did I call myself?

Despite the pain that the existence of the internet caused, it also brought me more guidance and community than any other resource. Not only was I introduced to the concept of being "woman aligned" but I also learned that nonbinary lesbians have existed forever. Gender and lesbianism have walked the path to liberation hand in hand. Stone butch lesbians have used he/him pronouns, femme lesbians like me have been using the singular "they" since before I was born and this comforted me greatly. I shouldn't need the historical background for a part of me to feel validated, but I'm honest enough to admit that new things terrify me. Not because of the change that they would bring, but because of the fear of those angry good ol' boys in the Facebook comments and stalking high school hallways with gunpowder smeared on their palm.

On top of all of this, I had to come to an understanding with my blackness as well. As most know, being queer and being black is a constant fight. For a long time in college, I had to choose between which I could express in a room. On the Black History Month planning committee, I was terrified to offer up the idea of having a discussion on the film Paris is Burning. In my LGBTQ group, I was too scared to offer up the idea of having a meeting on the topic of intersectionality, specifically black struggles. Because of historical context, there is a heavy weight that is put on the shoulders of black and LGBT people. There is pain being launched at us from both sides and I have found that the only way to soften the rock and the hard place is to pull them both together. There are voices of people with the same checkboxes as you, if not more. Listen to them. Delete the Facebook app from your phone and stop hate reading the opinions of those with no compassion for differences.

As I grow, I find that more and more boxes are being checked under my name. Whenever a new one arises, it is startling, but ultimately it is beautiful. Different combinations of checked boxes are what makes being human so magnificent.

The Poet Reacts To Misgendering Themself, Again

By T.C. Kody (they/them)

First, I do not apologize. I correct
myself, and move on. I do not think
of the hesitation I hear in my friends'
voices when they refer to me, at least,
when they are around me
or how that same pause exists, slowing
my thoughts my to-do lists my fun-
facts-about-myself. I do not think
of my body, or how this happens less
when I am clean shaven. I imagine
another self, an alternate me
who didn't question in the first place,
who was spanked and circumcised
and sent along his way never
thinking to think twice or differently
and I forgive that alternate me, I give
them a gift, the gift of the second
thought, and timelines merge. We own
this reflexive together, plural, even
and "they" does not feel like othering
myself, it feels like myself. I do
not apologize.

Them And Self

By Sandra Lopez (she/her & they/them)
Content warnings: *discussion of amatonormative standards*

Bisexual. Aromantic. Nonbinary.

A lot of discoveries about myself were made a bit "later than usual," compared to a lot of other people who knew exactly what they were doing at sixteen or at least before they left the safety of their home states and went to college to get up to whatever so-called "normal" college students do.

Well, I wasn't normal. And normal compared to who exactly? That's never been all that clear. "They/them" weren't an option back then. They weren't me. "They/Them" was meant for everyone else that I was afraid of, people who weren't my parents. Plus, I had no real concept of the possibility of not fitting the pronouns one was assigned at birth. I'm the child of immigrants from Mexico, firmly middle class, raised primarily in Chicago away from our relatives in Jalisco. Before anything else, I want to explain that the ones responsible for my voice, free and open in all its anxious shakiness and annoying pitchiness, are these immigrant parents. My father was responsible, never forbidding. My mother was strong, never submissive.

And I was an only child.

I played with "girly" things. I played house, I had Barbies and Ken dolls and had a healthy curiosity about their nude bodies. I wanted to be old enough to wear makeup so bad, ruining my mom's lipstick by running it all over my damn mouth like it actually looked good. To be fair, I was four, and I judge myself very harshly nowadays.

I was loud at home and at play, but, in all other respects, a "good girl," and I was a good girl all the way through college, which earned me depression and anxiety. I kept my sexuality to myself as I grew up, knowing the basics about sex and the way bodies worked and got my period at eleven. I was biologically female, and mentally prepping myself for the eventuality of having sex and babies.

Funny how those imaginings never actually included any particular kind of man.

Loud Me disappeared in middle school, replaced by Quiet and Resentful Me, bullied by the more socialized and determinedly feminine girls who made their friends easily while I kept my face hidden in a book. My anxiety and depression were there, and the only friends I made were kids like me, quiet and nerdy (and of indeterminate sexuality, compared to the firmly cis-hetero population around us).

My family didn't make things easier, but they didn't actively make things harder either. Mom made us go to church and there was no mention of anything especially liberal or modern to combat my very conservative paternal grandparents (my only living pair of grandparents). They grudgingly tolerated my aunts' gay friends and were pretty clear about how they felt about LGBT+ people in general. At the time I was having a bit of internal panic because my curiosity about boys was rapidly being outrun by my curiosity about GIRLS! GIRLS! GIRLS!

In high school, I called myself bicurious, but that was late in my senior year, after four years of going kissless and dateless. Honestly, I never exactly found the opportunity nor did I seek it. I was a Good Girl, avoiding the complications of sex and relationships and teen pregnancy. From what I'd seen relationships weren't that big a deal for me. Friends were more important (something these now former friends didn't seem to agree with).

As for my gender, I still thought I was a girl because that was what I had always been. I was going to wear a dress to my wedding and be judged by my 'she' pronouns. By the time I was eighteen my three older cousins already had kids. Supposedly it was my "turn" next, but my parents wanted me to go to college. I wanted to go to college and do something with my life.

So, I learned. I found pride in all my hard work and every accomplishment as those four golden years came and went, back when I thought I'd do something with my writing. My education on all things sex and gender went on, and it was around this time that I embraced the fact that I was incredibly bisexual and felt firmly "butch." Fuck homophobes and biphobes and traditional gender roles. It was my life and I wouldn't let my relatives' judgement affect me. Meanwhile, I was still quietly comparing myself to my prettier, more feminine cousins, absorbed in their relationships with good-looking men, which would make me wonder when something like that would happen for me. I was in an LGBT-friendly campus, my eyes on work and not particularly on anyone else, even if my imagination was pretty damn active and I was ready to GO.

But it looked like everyone else in the vicinity didn't get the memo, which has never really helped my fragile self-confidence. So, I was confident in my intelligence instead, in taking my time to jump headlong into having kids, especially after my younger cousins started getting married and having kids two seconds later. I waged a private conflict with amatonormativity, hating the assertion that my "better half" would bring me the ultimate happiness in the way that I felt a career and financial security would. Or single parenthood, since I really did and still do want to have kids one day.

So, my nonbinary identity conflicts with traditions. It wasn't always so surprising since a lot about me and the way I was raised went against tradition. I resented being told that because I was an only child I "owed" my parents plenty of grandkids to spoil. Of course, my parents told me to ignore that bullshit and focus on myself.

As it turns out "myself" included "they/them," the relieving pairing to the "she/her" I still carry with me, which is okay. It may be a remnant of my stubbornly gendered mother-tongue, but it's what's mine, kept close even as I claim the second set of pronouns, throwing the middle finger and a Spanish curse at anyone who wants me to follow some rigid set of rules when it comes to the complexities of gender and identity and sex. I'll wear my makeup, keep my hair long, wear a suit to my theoretical wedding and any other big events, and use the same supportive voice that my parents used as I grew up as I stand in front of them, out of the closet and still figuring out what I want to do in the future. Some things are just a bit clearer than others, but when it comes to me, myself, and my "them", I'll definitely have the words. I have plenty of them after all.

Skin-Deep Me

By Cassandra Jules Corrigan (any pronouns)

Sometimes my body is in mourning.
Sometimes I grieve for the skin I wasn't born in,
wishing my waist was thinner, my pants fit better,
agonizing over why my chest isn't flat, why my parts
don't match.
But other days my body is a celebration.
It's a fresh tattoo after years of wanting
and colored hair, all purple, blue, and green,
a declaration that what's mine is mine.
It's a map of stretch marks, shimmering white,
painted nails and scarlet lips.
It's acceptance of what I've been given,
what I've taken, and what I am living.
My beauty, my flaws, my skin-deep me.

Fig. 06. by Ronan Sullivan (they/them)

(Non)Existent

By Rune (they/them)

My gender does not exist.
It has no words, or lines, or shape;
it has nothing inherent about it except for me.
I don't like any pronouns offered,
and making up my own doesn't feel right.
So, I'll use they.
Sometimes, he.
I want a new name, but I'm not sure
how to exist outside my own.
The one assigned to me fits well enough.
Androgynous. Rolls off the tongue.
Easy to remember.
I look at new names and they
look like other people.
One day, I want to keep my name,
because not to feels foreign and wrong.
This name has worked so far, why try to fix it?
But other days are harder.
Everyone knows ___ is a she.
But they aren't. He isn't.
And this person feels glued to a name
and body that others define as female.
Some days I think a new name could really work.
I think a new name could help others cement
the idea of a new gender.
Not a new gender; no gender
or perhaps a gender constantly ebbing
and flowing through waves of androgyny.
It's not that I don't feel feminine:
masculinity just fits on me like silken sheets,
and lullabies sung by deep voices.

Androgyny does too; the idea slips
over my skin like a loving caress.
These things make me feel real.
Androgyny and masculinity are my dichotomy.
Femininity feels like a fraud,
because it tells the world I am a female.
It's rigid and pointed, like glass poking out of me.
It's a danger to myself and others;
it's invisible so no one sees.
It's supposed to look natural on me,
but I'm a model. I can make anything
look natural if I try hard enough.
Inside, I am a feminine other
but to allow this femininity to show
is to allow the world to force me into the
borders it constructed at my birth.
To allow this femininity to show is to endanger myself.
So, I feel the masculinity and androgyny
inside and embrace that.
I bind my chest and refuse to wear bras.
I sit with my legs wide open because someone
 like me has no use for the term "ladylike."
I wear skirts only around my lover,
because he understands.
I want to love myself
but I feel like Frankenstein's creature
made of parts that don't belong.
I want to love myself
but the world cannot see the gender inside me.
I want to love myself
but the gender within does not exist in a way
that anyone else can understand

My Name

By Artie Carden (they/them)

I don't hate my name, my birth name I mean.
The one given to me by who I love most,
the people I still hold close.
The name, that for 22 years, I have been.

But I struggle to understand I have a name.
Remembering it is strange.
Though the meaning is something I do acclaim,
I think it's time for a change.

So, I named myself.

It took 22 years to find something that works,
a name with just the right quirk.

I consciously practice; it has to be broken in.
I told a few people. I can't stop the grin
on my face when I order coffee or meet someone.
My heartbeat is drumming; I can still taste it on my
tongue.

I love the feel of it on my lips.
My name is Artie, and this is what fits.

The Positives And Negatives Of Being Agender

By Kayla Rosen (they/them)

When I first started identifying as agender, it was an entirely negative identity - not in the sense that it was bad, but in the sense of negative space. It was defined by absence, by the gender that wasn't there.

I'd been in college for about a year, and in that time, I'd learned from academic courses and slam poets that there were a million ways of defining gender, and there were genders besides female and male. The more I learned, the less I felt like I had a gender at all. Some people defined gender as chromosomes or genitals; that was obviously overly simplistic and cissexist. Other people explained their genders as a sense of sameness or kinship with others of a certain gender or as an affinity for certain types of presentations. That was fine for them, but it still didn't do anything for me. I felt more of a connection to women and nonbinary people than to men, but that was about sexism, not my own identity. I had preferred ways of dressing, talking, and moving through space, but those just felt like personal preferences. How could they be a gender presentation if they weren't about gender for me?

Most baffling to me were the people who said gender was a feeling. Okay, then what was it supposed to feel like? One of the best ways to describe my experience with trying to feel gender is the song "Nothing" from the musical A Chorus Line. In it, an auditioning performer sings about her experience at a performing arts high school where her instructor told her class to improvise being on a bobsled by feeling it: "They all felt something, but I felt nothing — except the feeling that this bullshit was absurd." For me, trying to conjure feelings of gender was equally futile. It felt like women were all in on some secret I'd missed. What were they feeling that I wasn't?

For a while, I kept trying to find ways to make my assigned gender work for me, especially after I told a cis friend I was questioning my gender and she said I was "too cis" to be nonbinary. In my philosophy of feminism class, we had discussed "woman" as an empty signifier, a word with no inherent meaning which could, therefore, mean anything. Maybe this apathetic nothingness inside me could be a kind of womanhood.

It didn't stick. I still felt like womanhood was something I was faking or failing to live up to. Maybe womanhood was an empty signifier, but most women didn't have to think of it that way to feel like women. Most women didn't have to think about it at all.

Finally, there was nothing left but to conclude that if it was so impossible for me to feel a gender, to connect to one in any way, I must not have one at all. A few years after the end of my friendship with the cis woman who had told me I couldn't be nonbinary, I tried tentatively using agender as my gender identity.

I wasn't sure about it at first. It felt like a new standard I would have to live up to when what I really wanted was to opt out of gender identity altogether. But in a world so defined by gender, I had to have something to say about my relation to it. At least there was a word for the apparent nonexistence of my gender.

I've been out as agender for four years now, and the label is working better for me than I expected. Claiming an identity defined by absence finally freed me from the pressure to "live up to" gender, to feel a gender or to pick out some of my existing feelings and force them to mean gender. Along the way, being agender has picked up positive meanings for me — in the sense of positive space, of presence, of having something, even if that something isn't gender.

People with genders feel and understand something I don't, but it's equally true that I feel and understand something they don't. As much as I can't imagine having a gender, they can't imagine not having one. I've found that many trans people, binary or not, with genders or without, can empathize with my experiences of negotiating my own identity and fighting for recognition. But in comparison to many cis people, who have never had to think so much about gender, I'm an expert about it. I can't relate to their perspectives, but I've investigated them with a diligence that cis people have never needed. It turns out that you can learn a lot about gender by not having one.

Being agender has also picked up more positive meanings for me as I've incorporated it into my art and advocacy. I created *Empty Gender/Full Bladder,* a zine about the difficulty of accessing all-gender bathrooms at my college as part of my activism for all-gender bathrooms in every building and a greater understanding of nonbinary people. My agender identity became a starting point for creative endeavors and building safer, more inclusive spaces. I've written poems about being agender that help me show myself that, as small and underground as it is for now, agender culture is possible. There is richness, texture, detail in the space where my gender isn't.

Finally, being agender is a point of connection with trans and nonbinary communities. In online spaces and in in-person groups like Seattle Nonbinary Collective, my identity and experiences as an agender person help me bond with people I respect and admire. Regardless of whether other group members share my exact label or relationship to gender, we're all dreaming and living possibilities beyond the gender binary. In loving nonbinary communities, my genderlessness is a valued part of our collective gender diversity.

Now, after several years of exploring, proclaiming, and fighting for my agender identity, being agender is a balance of presence and absence, a harmony of negative and positive space. I have no gender, no rules for how an agender person can or should live, no constant sense of falling short of my gender. I have agender insight, agender creativity, and agender community.

My gender is the weightless thrill of freefall. My gender is an open doorway to the future. My gender is a blank page that I have the freedom to fill how I want. My gender may be an absence, but it's anything but a lack.

Emergence

By A.E. Greythorne (they/them & she/her)
Content warnings: *homophobia, family issues, religion*

I know you wondered.
There's a reason
why you were so angry
when you found me cuddling
with my best friend.
We were children, only eight,
but you wondered.

I have been the squeaky wheel
and the black sheep since childhood.
I didn't want to be a girl.
Do you remember me telling you
that the doctor made a mistake?
That I was a boy?
That God put me in this body,
the one I had to hide
in baggy dresses
three sizes too big,
the one that didn't do what I wanted it to,
the one that bled
and curved
and didn't fit me
by mistake?

I didn't want to be like this.
I begged God to take it away.
Don't make another mistake,
I told him
for there was no greater sin
than being a mistake

in the eyes of your parents.

I carried my Bible with me at all times
with my notebook
and hand-wrote the words of God
whenever I was inclined to sin.
When I thought about her,
I wrote Colossians;
when I envisioned her in those jeans,
I wrote Ephesians;
I wondered what her lips felt like
I wondered if she might love me
or if she might think of me late at night
watching the fan blades slowly turn
wishing they were pages in a fairy tale turning
into happily ever after for us.
When I thought of these things,
I wrote Philippians.

The pressure built up too great
for my masquerade
and sooner or later,
the mask had to come off.
The disappointment had to be faced.
Your greatest fears had to be realized
and your darkest secret
lay uncloaked before you.

I was the shame,
the squeaky wheel,
the black sheep,
the sinner.

But in reality, I did you a favor -

I came out of the closet
so, I wouldn't have to always be
the skeleton in yours.

Can You See Me?

By Keshav Kant (he/him & she/her)
Content warnings: *misgendering, transphobia,
colonialism*

I'll bet you my student loans that every queer person
has heard the question "Are you… you know…?"
whispered to them in hushed tones. Our lives are like a
high-risk trivia game. "When did you know you weren't
straight?", "So are you like trans now?" "Will you get the
surgery?", "How can you be gay? You're Indian!" (and
yes, I'm serious about that last one).

Even when we are represented in the media it's
through a very narrow lens. When people think of the
LGBTQ+ community they think of white able-bodied cis
gay men and women. Being queer is often associated
with whiteness and The West. and being a queer person
of colour means you're never truly represented
anywhere. The "Colourblind" West can't see the
radiance of my melanin, and my home had its queer
history so violently erased by colonialism that they
refuse to acknowledge that it was even there to begin
with.

I ended up living a half-life where I could never
truly be my authentic self. When I'm rolling through the 6
with my queer friends, or with my fellow ethnics or even
my ethnic queers, they don't completely understand.
They are as sympathetic as they can be, and they are
always supportive of my self-expression, but they don't
totally understand.

I live in a world that thinks my identity is a quirk,
something made up on the fringes of the internet.
"You're just confused", "That's a Tumblr thing, right?",
"Your entire generation just loves to feel special." No!

No, I don't! I'm just sick and tired of living my life in a claustrophobic little box because of what's between my legs. People like me had existed happily for millennia before it was taken from us by colonialism! Around the globe people who were neither men or women used to thrive. The Sht of Ancient Egypt, wíŋkte of Native peoples, Muxe people of Oaxaca and my people: the Hijras of India.

I am part of one of the oldest living communities of trans/intersex/gender diverse people on Earth. We have many names and faces but one thing remains the same: we have been here just as long as you have. Throughout Indian history, the Kinner (our proper name, as Hijra is a reclaimed slur) had a high standing in society. We were considered magical beings with the power to bless or curse a child or a marriage. We were dancers, singers and performers who received patronage from royalty. We served as their protectors, their confidants, their advisers, and even shared their beds. Tales of our existence are even in the Hindu epic 'Mahabharata'. Arjuna, one of the five Pandava Princes' was said to have been a Kinner. He's hailed as one of India's greatest warriors.

But you would never have guessed that we used to hold such high stations of power and influence if you looked at my people today. Thanks to the rigid rule of Colonial Britain and the lasting effects of their empire, having a Hijra child is seen as a blight on the honour of a family. Parents of intersex kids weep and lament at the shame that their child would bring to them. Most don't even bring the child home, through the child is taken in by the local Hijra community and raised as their own in commune like homes where mothers look after their adoptive children, generally scraping by doing odd jobs, begging or sex work.

73

I had the good fortune of not being visibly a Hijra. I was the first-born son to newlyweds, the pride of the family and the apple of everyone's eye. I got to stay with my biological family and be loved. Even when I dressed in my mother's heels and sari it was just a cute thing kids did, when I asked everyone to call me a girl it was seen as a joke, but no one actually saw and heard what I was asking for.

I wanted my femininity to be seen, to be recognized. I wasn't a girl, but I definitely wasn't a boy so why couldn't everyone see what I saw? Why could they feel what I felt when I looked in the mirror?

I learned that they didn't want to, so I started to bury it eventually. To hide my dysphoria under big ill-fitting clothes, to hide my confusion and dislike of my own body under the guise of teenage angst and anger. I rebelled in little ways when I could, such as shaving my face so close that I cut myself all just to not have a beard. I shunned all of the things boys were supposed to do and instead threw myself into art, cooking and music. And I surrounded myself with girls my age because that's where I felt most comfortable.

But it didn't last long. Those were the darkest years of my life. Every moment spent wrapped in hatred, anger and sadness. I hurt myself and those around me. Those wounds have only just begun to heal now that I have let myself be my true self. When I finally embraced all of me the pain eased and the weight that I walked with lifted. My terrible posture got slightly better and I stood tall for the first time. Head held high, towering above all the others as I strut my already 6'3 self, down the street in a pair of platform sneakers.

Only after I stopped giving myself razor burns and grew out my magnificent lumberjack beard, did I start to love my face. When I painted my nails a peacock blue, I saw the beauty of my long-fingered pianist's fingers. After I grew out my hair and let it curl and twist to its heart content, I noticed that it didn't need to be bright purple for it to be stunning. It took nearly twenty-one years, decades spent on a lonely rock in this corner of space to realize that I can be me and people will just have to deal with it. Just like people dealt with it for centuries before the colonizers came and ruined it for all of us.

I am a gay man, a queer Indo-Canadian, a Kinner. A Hijra. I'm the magical being who danced and sang for royalty. A protector to the people I love, a confidant they trust with their lives, an advisor they listen to in times of need, the lover who they marvel at when we share a night. I see myself and it's about damn time that you saw me too.

They

By Rain Scher (they/them)

This is a poem about pronouns,
Habits, attitudes and opinions,
Experiences and behaviours. Do
You know what I'm talking about?

The intention of using 'they' seems to cause a
Heart racing with anxiety but
Everyone does it all the time.
You've probably done it at least once today.

Thoughtful usage is somehow harder but
Having to ask for it is worse.
Eventually it gets easier to say,
You just practice.

They say "can't you just
Hide this, quiet this.
Erase yourself a little more,
You'll make it easier for everyone else."

They say, "it's not grammatically correct!"
How often are most people incorrect?
Every day, every hour, every five fucking minutes
Yet my existence is offensive to your grammar?

There are no reasons for language to be this way.
History tells us nonbinary people are not new -
English was constructed out of oppressive systems.
Yes, language is powerful, but not unchangeable.

They use singular 'they' all the time.
How can it be harder to do on purpose?
Erasure hurts, misgendering hurts more.
Yes, my preference is respect.

There are more than two genders.
Hormones and body parts are not all we are.
Each of us is unique and individual
Yet this dominant culture tells us to choose.

The times we assert ourselves make room for others.
Harbingers of a paradigm shift, we embody alchemy and
Embodying alchemy, we subvert cis-het patriarchy
Yelling truth to power.

Fig. 07 by A. Alderman (ae/aer)

77

Are You Even Human?

By Charlie B. (they/them)
Content warnings: *misgendering, aphobia*

Ever since I was old enough to buy my own clothes, I knew that I fit somewhere outside the limiting gender binary. I had been moulded into shape by my parents who after having three sons, just wanted a little girl they could buy pretty dresses. The first chance I got, I cut away all that long hair they had wanted for me, threw out any skirts or dresses and embraced oversized hoodies with skinny jeans. I was determined to run as far away from gender roles as I could.

These days, I am comfortable expressing myself in a variety of ways. Clothing has no gender, after all. It has no bearing on my identity. There is some irony that my realisation that I was something other than what I was assigned at birth came from a comment made by my father, who desperately held on to anything that tied me to femininity. It was an offhand comment, one that implied that I was neither "boy nor girl", that led to me scouring the internet in hopes of finding other people like me. I owe a lot to that search.

Agender and non-binary are both terms I hold close to my heart in defining who I feel I have always been. However, my questioning of my identity did not end there.

The first time I considered asexuality was when I got my first real boyfriend at sixteen. By then I was comfortable with my non-binary identity, I thought the hardship of getting other people to understand and accept me was over for the most part. It helped that by then I had surrounded myself with friends in the LGBTQ community. My ex-boyfriend was a nice guy, we had been good friends before he asked me out. I said yes, naturally, as I could not see a reason why I should have said no. He was my friend, he was funny and kind, we stayed up late chatting and flirting a little. I thought that when we started dating, something would just change in me and I would feel the way that all the protagonists in romantic movies do. I even told him that I was waiting for that while we were dating.

But it never came.

At first, it seemed like we were on the same page about sex. We talked about it, as friends we had always been very open about it. I told him I had little interest in having it, and he agreed with me. Looking back, I think he was just saying whatever would make me happy. He always was a bit of a "yes man". It became clear that he was seeking more physical intimacy than I was comfortable with. He always respected my wishes to slow down, even when I asked for him to not touch me at all unless I initiated that contact. I couldn't quite place the anxiety. Just his presence made me nervous and not in the fluttery butterflies feeling I had heard so much about. I did not want to cuddle, I did not want to kiss, I did not want to be touched at all. Not by him, not by anyone. Things began adding up in the brain. I had never had a crush on anyone, I felt no desire to be with anyone. Happiness could be found in other things like sleeping in on a rainy day with my dog curled up at the end of my bed. A romantic relationship was the last thing I needed to feel happy. While I had an emotional connection with my best friend, there was no need for anything else.

I sometimes wondered if my being agender and my asexuality were connected. My ex asked too. I wondered if this dysphoria I was feeling with my body was somehow interfering with my drive to have sex.

Was I so uncomfortable with myself that the idea of being in a relationship was repulsive to me? Agender, asexual, aromantic: were all these labels I had suddenly attached to myself somehow causing each other?

Ultimately, no. Those questions are not tied to a good place in my life and it was a dangerous mindset. My relationship with sex had less to do with my body and more to do with attraction, or lack of in my case. I am very open about sex, including discussing and writing about it, sometimes I even desire it. I hunger, but there is simply nothing on the menu that I want to eat. However, this does not bother me I live my life happily without a romantic or sexual partner, and comfortable with my gender identity.

It was this desire for different things that ultimately led to me breaking up with my ex and I have not looked back since. However, even despite how comfortable I felt with myself, it did not stop future platonic relationships from taking unpleasant turns. Agender, asexual, aromantic: all terms that often have been to be explained whenever I come out to someone new. It gets tiresome, but luckily most approach it with an open mind. It has even led to friends discovering things about themselves that they did not realise earlier. Sadly, there are always going to be some who approach things they do not understand with bigotry and aggression. People have laughed in my face, asked me how I could possibly live my life without sex or a relationship at all as that was what made people human, told me I should just "pick a gender" because there was no such thing as non-binary. Too many times I have been compared to plants, to things as far away from human as they can because imagining being devoid of anything that they consider a necessity to function as a human being is a leap they are unwilling to take.

These identities are something that have greatly affected my life. I hope for a future where marginalised identities can live free of bigotry. For all the times I have been asked to just pick a "normal" gender, told that I would eventually find the person who would set me right, I have found a person who accepts my they/them pronouns with open arms, who assures me that I am not broken in any way. There is happiness to be found - you just have to be willing to look for it.

This Or That

By Mel G. Cabral (they/them)
Content warnings: *biphobia, colonialism*

"Here's the thing," my co-worker had huffed. "I don't believe in bisexuals. It's either you're straight or you're gay. That's it."

I shrank in my seat as I mumbled into my mug: "But… I'm bisexual."

An uncomfortable silence filled the room. I was left feeling invisible as I quietly sipped my coffee, wondering if anybody would address that a bisexual did, in fact, exist in the very same office. For a while, I tried to process this experience by joking that I was the ghost of bisexuality. Funnily enough, the same officemates started believing there was a ghost in the office. I eventually figured out that because I was so short, they could only see the top of my head from behind one of the cubicles. It was this or that: there's a ghost or not ghost at all. The notion that I could have been standing there didn't occur to them; my existence couldn't possibly have been an option.

I've lived most of my life with these "in-between" identities, even if I didn't have the vocabulary for them at the time. I didn't swing one way in terms of romantic attraction and I never felt wholly like a girl, but it also felt wrong to be called a boy. As a result, I spent most of my childhood being called a tomboy, but that wasn't it either. Besides, being a tomboy was seen as undesirable, especially in the strictly conservative Roman Catholic school I grew up in.

Unfortunately, we were never taught that there could be any labels for "in-between" or even "neither." There was only boy or girl, straight or gay, religious or atheist. There were no markers that assured me that what I felt was real. Some well-intentioned friends told me that labels didn't matter, but that was easy for them to say, given that they already had labels which suited them. It took time for me to find like-minded people, to find out that there were labels that coincided with how I felt on the inside.

There are days when I feel more pansexual than bisexual or even times when I feel asexual. Once I was a tomboy, then a gender non-conforming woman, then genderqueer. I realized soon after that there were days when I felt more like a 'female,' so I identified as genderfluid, then genderqueer and genderfluid, with a healthy mix of "do I count as trans?" and "am I actually male?" mixed in. Yet using 'female' felt off, 'male' even more so; 'non-binary female' or 'genderqueer female' sometimes felt okay (but not quite). I now identify mainly as non-binary, but it still shifts around.

Fig. 08 by Shunamara "Mars" Trippel (they/them

Regardless, people still tell me: "you can't know that for sure" or "that isn't real" or "are you sure you aren't [x] instead?"

My race is not exempt from this type of interrogation, either. I have had many an awkward transaction with fruit vendors who immediately speak to me in English, assuming I am Chinese, Korean, or even Japanese, then being taken aback when I respond in Tagalog. There is a certain loneliness to feeling like a stranger to your own mother country, the only homeland you've ever known. Yet I never grew up with any sort of Chinese upbringing; I lack the background that most Chinese-Filipinos experience.

I may be one of many in this odd position of technically being "Filipino-American," yet the only life I have known is that of a Filipino, perhaps not "born" here but certainly raised since infanthood in the Philippines. As a young child, I was worried that I would be forced to choose between Filipino and US citizenship once I hit the age of 18. It felt like another choice being forced upon me: this or that. Fortunately, dual citizenship became an option, but I still remember feeling like I was betraying my country by taking US citizenship if I had no other choice.

In both blood and lived experience, I relate more to the 'Filipino' and 'Filipina' identities as they are understood here in the Philippines. However, even identifying as 'Filipino' has been rife with uncertainties. It can be exasperating to try and explain this to foreigners; more than once we have been jokingly called "the Mexicans of Asia." When it comes to our culture, it's difficult to identify which parts are 'purely' Filipino and which parts were inspired by outside influence, whether it's our architecture, cuisine, or even our religious beliefs. Our language also has elements from Malay,

Chinese, English, and Spanish, to name a few. Thus, a common refrain: "what is 'Filipino?'" It could be a multitude of things: our hospitality, our resilience, our kapatiran. But what does it really mean to be Filipino?

In fact, even the name 'Philippines' is derived from the name of the Spanish king who ruled at the time of our colonization. I recall a petition not too long ago for the 'Philippines' to be changed to 'Malaya' (freedom) to supposedly re-align with our pre-colonial roots. But the thing is that we cannot deny our colonial history; attempting to erase it completely ignores the malleable, adaptive nature of the Filipino identity, and the impact said colonization has had on our people and culture. We are Filipino even with our colonial history, not in spite of it.

The same 'decolonization' sentiment gave rise to the term Filipinx in recent years. Filipinx is a term created by those in the diaspora in an attempt to decolonize the identity and make it more inclusive for those outside the gender binary. Indeed, Filipino pre-colonial culture had a rich history of gender fluidity, examples of which including the babaylan, a female figure of authority and a highly respected spiritual and political leader. However, the role was not strictly limited to women; men could also take on the heavily admired role of babaylan. There also existed powerful female deities such as Malitong Yawa. Many of our mythological figures were not assigned specific genders at all, including the diwata. When Spain colonized the Philippines, all these were deemed unacceptable according to their pre-conceived notions of the world. Thus, our culture—and especially our language—began to change, as influenced by Spain: the babaylan were called 'witches', the 'yawa' in Malitong Yawa came to mean 'devil', and 'diwata' came to be associated with female deities.

Spanish is inherently a heavily gendered language. I, personally, was perplexed by the idea of 'male' and 'female' words: words ending in -o for male, -a for female. This was nothing like the gender-neutral Tagalog language I grew up with where there is no "he/him" or "she/her," only "siya"; no "his" or "her," only "kanya," no "wife" or "husband" only "asawa", no "daughter" or "son" only "anak." Words are not inherently male or female; there is no need to use different versions of the same word. Even the term 'Filipino' has been challenged by some, alleging that it is a gendered term that is only inclusive to those who identify as male. However, going back to our rich history, 'Filipino' is actually a gender-neutral term. According to Donna Denina of Gabriela Seattle, it was "born out of a nationalized unity to fight against a common oppressor... it is, therefore revolutionary to identify as Filipino." Filipinx as a term thus came under fire for appearing to idealize indigenous concepts of gender and also forgetting the historical context as to how we came to identify as Filipino. But more importantly, how indigenous groups grapple with their racial, cultural, and gender identities are uniquely theirs to experience; we cannot claim to have the same lived experiences as them nor can we take certain aspects of their experiences to fit ours. At the same time, however, I cannot deny those in the diaspora their unique experiences when it comes to finding an identity that suits them. That's the thing: there is no one size fits all and that's okay.

All of these discourses have helped me to better understand my own identity. Indeed, my identity may not coincide with what is understood by others, but it is a lived experience that is uniquely mine. I discovered that using 'non-binary Filipina' to describe myself fit me like a glove. I have wrestled with so much confusion over my own seemingly contradictory identities: how could someone genderqueer possibly be comfortable with a seemingly feminine racial identifier? For a long time, this acceptance of a 'gendered' term made me question whether I was truly non-binary, or if I was what a handful of people from the trans community had called the 'theys': by their definition, 'supposedly' genderqueer AFAB people who can try on the privilege of being female whenever being genderqueer became too inconvenient. It was through a lesbian Catholic friend of mine, who had been told by an extremist male atheist that it was impossible for her to be a lesbian and Catholic at the same time, that I became more confident in my identity. She said she could be both. It made me decide that I can reconcile my identity with my seemingly contradictory experiences and beliefs.

I've come to learn that certain sections of the LGBTQIA+ community believe that a non-binary identity requires a complete rejection of either male or female identities (and if you identified as either, even if only occasionally, then you weren't really non-binary). However, much in the same way that 'Filipinx' and 'Malaya' are problematic for their erasure of our history, so, too, can I not reject the lived experience I have had as a Filipina, initially assigned female at birth, in a highly conservative Roman Catholic South East Asian country. As much as accepting my Filipina identity does not mean entirely rejecting the traces of other cultures upon our own, realizing and choosing a non-binary identity does not require an erasure of my AFAB past; neither does it mean a rejection of the already gender-neutral term 'Filipino' and the implications of the term 'Filipina.'

All of these are part of what makes me who I am; I am not only the past or the present. I am not only this or that. I can be both, I can be neither, I can be something else entirely.

When The Things We Love Don't Love Us Back

By K.C. (they/them)

Content warnings: *homophobia, lesbophobic slurs, family issues*

There are things that we love that don't "love us back."
In the romance world, unrequited love is beautiful and
tragic. It's no different for queer people who love things
that don't love and nurture their queerness. As a queer
POC, there is a list, far too long to write about, of things,
people and places that I love with everything in my soul
which don't love me back.

My Home

The south is viewed either entirely negatively or entirely
positively. It gets a lotta mixed reviews from actual
southerners, but no group is more conflicted about how
they feel than southern born queers like me. Funnily
enough, most people don't think there are queer people
in the south. I am proof of the contrary. Growing up in
the south I was taught that everything was supposed to
be a certain way. Everyone was cis and straight and
followed all the rules or, so I thought. I did what I was
told for years. I crossed my legs when I wore a skirt. I
dressed as femininely as possible. I acted like the girl I
was told I was supposed to be. I had crushes on boys
like I was supposed to. I had a crush on a new boy
practically every week. I never actually dated or flirted
with boys because that made it too real for me. I was in
6th when I first considered that I might be bi and that
scared me. I even turned down a request from a boy
that asked for my number my junior year. In my head, I
thought "If a girl asked for my number, I would give it to

her". That thought scared me even more. I wasn't following the rules this place laid out for me. I was starting to reject the south and it was starting to reject me back.

My Mom

I'm in college and I talk on the phone with my mom every Sunday. She doesn't know I'm queer or that I have a crush on a girl. When I finally tell her, I think our conversations will stop feeling like small talk - no depth all surface. The opposite happens. It feels like now we're avoiding my girlfriend in every conversation. When I bring her up, she goes silent and then continues the conversation like I said nothing at all. A year later it's more of the same. I have a new girlfriend but her attitude towards my queerness still hasn't changed. She acts like it's not a thing. We have awkward conversations about my love life where she tries her best to understand and relate to me. I've given up on sharing that aspect of my life with her. She'll never get it.

My Family

Casual homophobia is common in my family and never made me feel like I could confidently be myself around them. Before I go off to college my grandmother tells me a story. She talks about a girl at her church that came out to her family as gay. Her family apparently "accepted her" but still prayed for her to change. As if it's that simple. A few years after she came out as gay, she is now getting married to a guy. My bi ass is sitting there half believing and half not believing her story. Bisexuality doesn't exist in her mind and the fact that it was never brought up during this whole conversation discouraged me from coming out more than her little story did. I pushed that idea far out of my mind. She told me this story never considering I might be gay myself. I bet the thought never even crossed her mind.

My Body
Whenever I look in the mirror, I never know how I will feel about what I see. Some days I love my curvy shape and big stomach. Others, I wish my chest was far smaller than it is, and I think my shape is far too feminine. I know I can never pull off the kind of androgynous look I want with my body shape. The phrase "I love my body" comes with a 'but' on those days. My body is the part of myself I'm constantly fighting against. Nothing ever seems right. On my demigirl and gender-neutral days I love everything about myself but other days I pick apart the characteristics that I blame for why I can't pass as my true gender. I blame my body for existing as it does. For not morphing itself into something I can love no matter what gender I am. Being genderfluid is like constantly being at war with an enemy and a lover simultaneously. The body that causes me dysphoria is the same body that allows me to feel the sunlight and the soft touches from loved ones. My body is both my biggest enemy and my best friend.

My Religion
When I was a little kid, I was very religious. I believed in Christianity as much as I believed in God. Most religious folks know that's the first mistake I made. I didn't realize what I had done wrong until later. I was a teenager when I learned the error of my ways. It started small. Nasty looks turned into little offhand comments. Eventually, the religion that I loved so much turned into judgment that I subjected myself to every week. They could tell I didn't fit in and I didn't know how to convince

them otherwise. I loved that religion and God desperately but that didn't matter to them. At the end of the day, I was too queer and not modest enough for them.

My Blackness

I'm putting on my black girl performance around my family. My full black accent is turned on high. I'm having a good time with my little cousin until suddenly she starts talking about "curious dykes" in college. My heart almost stops as I struggle to find the words to defend them. I tell her she shouldn't say that word because it's a slur. That's all I can say over and over again. The conversation continues as if nothing happened. Then I remember how often this happens. How often my identities turn against me. How much I can't forget that I live in this black, queer, woman-perceived body no matter how much I want to.

My Femininity

I'm a proud nonbinary femme. I scream that label confidently from the rooftops. I love how feminine I am. It comes naturally to me. During the short time I identified as a lesbian I never felt like I was allowed to claim the femme label. It was almost an alien idea to me. When I became aware of the nonbinary community, I immediately clung to the femme label to pair with my newfound nonbinary one. Even so, there are days where I resent my femininity. I hate how it feels to be misgendered because of it. I hate how it causes people to assume I'm faking the whole nonbinary thing. I hate how it induces my dysphoria on the days my gender isn't connected to the binary at all. It's hard because something that means so much to me also hurts me all at the same time.

Reform Trans

By Mike Levine (they/them)
***Content warning:** internalised transphobia*

The thing I love most about being Jewish is that it encourages questions. Doubt isn't a threat to my faith, it's a central part of it. I don't think about G-d a lot (Hebrew School reflexes keep me from spelling that word out), but I think about being Jewish all day.

As much as I love Judaism, I used to get really self-conscious around Orthodox Jews. "There goes a failed Jew," I'd imagine them thinking, deducting Jew Points for my shaved head, rap t-shirt, and lack of hat. They were much more Jewish; therefore, I was much less. They had dignity and a directness of purpose that I could never touch. They were full-time, I was part-time. From the outside, at least in my imagination, they seemed so sure of themselves. No doubt at all. I couldn't identify with that, and it took a long time for me to let go of the notion of being more or less Jewish than they were.

Reform Judaism taught me that I am fully Jewish. It didn't rest on any one qualification. I didn't have to know every Yiddish term my grandfather threw out, or every word in a Hebrew blessing mumbled once a year. I don't go to services, but I've spent most of my life teaching in Hebrew School classrooms. Education is the core of my Jewish practice, but I'm still Jewish without it. I'm Jewish because I feel it. I'm Jewish because I love it. I'm Jewish because something in my heart says "yes."

A few months into exploring what I thought of as a "cross-dressing fetish", I started getting really self-conscious around trans women. I felt like I was making a game of something they took seriously. They were a lifestyle; I was an amateur hobbyist. I almost wanted it to be, as someone I heard second-hand put it, "just a sex thing." If it was a fetish, I could keep it private and it wouldn't have any unforeseen implications on the rest of my life. It made sense to me that I'd want to wear dresses in front of my partner - it was exciting! But it didn't explain why I'd put them on when she wasn't home, or how calm it made me feel. More questions.

My big breakthrough happened because of a Twitter thread by Julia Kaye - 'how did you know you were trans?' She took pains to include nonbinary people in it, and it was a revelation for me. I didn't think nonbinary was fully trans. I had always thought trans meant strongly identifying with the "opposite" gender instead of what it actually is, not identifying with your assigned gender. Here was a very clear answer: I don't fully identify as a woman, but I've NEVER felt comfortable with being male. So I was trans. I called up my partner at the time, proudly announced "Hey, I'm trans!" and broke down immediately. It was a good cry, the best kind, the one where you're more relieved than you were ever scared. She wasn't surprised at all. She loved me, and she knew where my heart was.

I changed my pronouns in my Twitter bio, the traditional first step. I pored over an intense email to my family. I explained I was something I didn't totally understand and hoped they would try to. Then more questions came, hard and fast. Would I change my pronouns? My voice? Could I find acceptance in the queer community without a septum piercing? Would I need surgery or hormones? Did I even want them? Was any given stab of anxiety actually dysphoria? Should I shave my legs? Did I want to wear makeup? That was months ago, and I still only have answers to two of them. What I'm trying to do is get more comfortable with the questions.

And that's where Judaism helps. The way I see it, the trans women I look up to are orthodox trans, and I'm reform trans. Neither of us are more or less trans, and they were never judging me. (The gatekeeping was coming from inside the house!) I can choose to participate in any one gendered behavior or not and this can change over time. I can doubt what I want or what I need, but I don't have to doubt who I am. I'm nonbinary because I feel it. I'm nonbinary because I love it. I'm nonbinary because, when presented with a path that was neither male nor female, something in my heart said "yes."

"It's A Girl"

By Katie S. (they/them)

Content warnings: cissexism, transphobia, positive use of "cunt"

One Tuesday, in 1987,
a doctor presented my mother with a baby,
and said: "Congratulations! It's a girl!"
27 years later, I said: "Maaaybe not."

Not everyone was friendly.

"But Katie's a girl's name," they said
and I shot back, "And if a celebrity calls their son Katie
next week, will it be unisex then?"
They didn't have an answer for that.

"But you've got long hair."
Incredulously, I ask:
"Have you NEVER seen a metal dude?"
That's different, they say. But they don't know why.

They insinuate that gender is defined by mammary
glands and genitals.
But neither my boobs nor my cunt make me a girl.
I'm not a girl, and this is my body
so, it cannot be a girl's body.

"Why do you wear makeup?"
Because I like colours and glitter
and painting rainbows on my face.
I like how lipstick defines my lips, and the way it smears
when I kiss.

A boy taught me how to do it.
The same boy who taught me to walk in heels.
So, you can STUFF your stereotypes.
This is my makeup… not a girl's.

"You're so difficult!"
Hold on, hold on.
You think asking society not to gender me
based on what's between my legs is difficult for you?

I'll tell you what's difficult.
Difficult is existing in a world alongside Piers Morgan
and denizens of Reddit
with their 'attack helicopters'.

I'm not difficult for saying I'm not a girl.
I'm just trying to find my place
in this world.
I'm they. I'm me.

Fig. 09 by Andy Passchier (they/them)

The Only Binary I Need

By Jo Newton (they/them)
Content warnings: *eating disorder*

The room is cold. Or maybe I'm cold and the room is a normal temperature. It's hard to tell the difference these days.

There is a sign on one of the cupboards that reads "Let me know if I'm using the wrong pronouns." But that requires some chutzpah, an amount of courage that has disappeared along with my energy and much of who I am as a person. I'm here trying to claim all of it again.

I had a restriction-based eating disorder. Eating disorders tend to rob you of your agency and make you feel isolated and like nobody understands your experiences. I'm also nonbinary. Being nonbinary tends to make you feel isolated and like nobody - or at least nobody who exists within the gender binary - understands your experiences. Being a nonbinary person with an eating disorder is an isolating experience unlike any other.

Most resources for recovery are geared towards women and girls. Most resources for people who are sick and want to stay sick are also geared towards women and girls. Rarely, these resources will mention men and the importance of being gender-inclusive by including "men and women." But they almost never use truly gender-neutral language, and I've never found one that has actually, specifically acknowledged nonbinary people. When you're in such a vulnerable place, with a mental illness that only wants to find ways to convince you to starve yourself to death, exclusion from resources that typically provide hope has the potential to sever your last lifeline.

I remember thinking that if I didn't eat as much, there wouldn't be as much fat on my hips and I wouldn't look so effeminate. I remember looking at lists of reasons to recover, seeing people list "your breasts will get bigger" and immediately closing the tab. Weight loss, in my head, was a ticket to androgyny, to a body that didn't trigger my dysphoria at every turn.

Yet I found myself still with the dysphoria that I had had before but also with newfound anxiety about my body. I hated my hips, but I also hated my thighs. I hated my breasts, but I also hated my stomach. I hated how wide my upper arms were, and the fact that I could not wrap my fingers around them. To be thin is to be androgynous, I told myself, and being androgynous will solve my dysphoria. It will solve all my problems.

Except that it didn't solve my problems. Not only did I wind up with more to hate, I also wound up with less of me to give. Sure, in my case - which is not true for everybody - I lost weight. But I also lost energy, security, friendships, trust in myself and from others, my health, the ability to juggle all the things I was doing and joy. I became a shell of a person, a ghost among the living, even more othered than I was before. I noticed how much people bond over food, and how uncomfortable I was in any situation like that. I realized how much people talked about body shapes as gendered and how the one I was trying to starve myself into was just as gendered as the one as I was trying to leave behind. I existed in this space of a half-life: I clearly wasn't dead, but I wasn't living either.

Most of my life is lived outside of binaries. I'm nonbinary, which is the first thing people think of when talking about social binaries. I'm invisibly disabled meaning I look able-bodied but I'm really not - and yet because of this, I fit in neither place. I'm ethnically Jewish but not religiously so, so I find I've got myself teetering on the edge of the community, one foot in, one foot out.

Ironically enough, it was a binary way of thinking that saved me. I realized that there are really only two outcomes to eating disorders: recovery or death. There is no way to continue living in the half-life forever. There is no nonbinary equivalent to life or death: you must choose and please choose life.

As it turns out, the office is, in fact, cold but it's also me. I know this because I am cold everywhere: in this office, in classrooms, in my bed under three blankets and with a heating pad, at work and in the shower with the water turned as hot as it will go. But the fact that the office is also objectively cold (or at least the nurse thinks it is cold and adjusts the temperature) makes me relieved. At least, this time, it is not only due to starving myself so badly that I cannot produce enough heat. This time, it's normal.

For some reason, this knowledge - that someone else has the same experiences as me in this moment, however small, that someone else feels the room is cold - is enough for me to promise myself that I will correct the nurse when she misgenders me. And she does, and I do. She corrects herself. I see a world of confusion in her eyes, but she does not ask, and simply respects me. She is not here to judge. She is only here to help.

Damn those too binary recovery sites. Damn the knowledge that eating more will give me bigger breasts. Damn it all. There is someone else who had the same

101

experience as me just for a moment, and there is someone who is compassionate and only here to help, and damn the eating disorder itself. The only binary I need to acknowledge and be a part of is the life or death binary, and, damn it, I am going to choose life.

She asks me to step on the scale and I do. She writes down the number and I sit down and wait for her to take my blood pressure, but she doesn't. So instead, I ask her, "Can you help me choose life?"

My evidence is anecdotal, and my research is conducted only through searching YouTube videos and Tumblr posts, but it seems that there's a higher ratio of people with eating disorders in the trans community than in the general population. I don't know what this breakdown looks like among binary trans versus nonbinary people, but regardless it seems like it affects our community at an unfairly high degree.

Starving yourself (or any of the other ways eating disorders manifest; not all of them are restriction-based, but I write what I know) will not solve your dysphoria. Restricting will not help you find where you belong outside the binary; nor will it allow you to fit back inside it if that's not where you belong. An eating disorder tells you that it will solve all your problems but a life without an eating disorder is open and free and binary-less. It's a world of options, choices, discovery and adventure. A world with an eating disorder is one where you're always backed into a corner and, every day, you make one choice over and over again: do I walk towards death or towards life?

I know it feels so, so, so isolating to be in the midst of an eating disorder, especially while nonbinary. I know you feel there are no resources, and I know you feel like you are alone. But I promise that someone else in the room feels cold. They might be nonbinary, and they might not be. But at this point, that doesn't really matter. What matters is you find some reason, whatever it is, to get better. Because you deserve a life of fullness and joy.

Abandon all binaries. Choose recovery.

Remember The Twilight

By Mx. Rowan (they/them)

Normally, I am proud of my people.

I'll proudly proclaim how Jews have six genders - not two
- and how I'm historically non-binary, not modernly,
thank you very much.

But Christians are no longer the only ones who are binary.

Everything in Hebrew is gendered:
this she, that she, gave she, received he, flowers he,
from she, together he and she. There is no they.

We are people of the book, but even words on a page
are divided in holy balance between ink and paper,
words and negative space. But it takes more than ink
and paper to make a book.

The days are marked into day and night, night and day,
dark and light.

It seems we have forgotten: our liminal spaces are
sacred.

Twilight is holy. The space between letters is holy.
We dress our scrolls and our books as well as ourselves
because beauty is a command, a mitzvot,
and we kiss their bound spines when they fall
and raise them to the heavens for blessing.

But when I expressed "I exist", I felt like a not-quite-yet-convert,
an outsider to my own people - like I had to be denied three
times before I could find a rabbi who said: "I see you."

We have lost our liminal spaces and holy in-betweens.
Do not forget the twilight.
Because my people may have become binary

but I am not.

Betwixt And Between

By Morgan Peschek (they/them)
Content warnings: *internalised transphobia*

My high school required that girls wear skirts.

Not just any skirts, oh, no. I went to a high school in England, where uniforms are the norm, and a fee-paying high school, at that – so strict uniforms were the norm. They required that my parents shell out around £40 for a stiff tube of grey, scratchy fabric with a polyester lining that I can only describe as feeling 'slimy'. It fell just above my knees and moved too much when I walked, except at the waist, where it didn't seem to move enough.

I hated it so passionately that my mother wrote to the school to request that I be allowed to wear trousers. A response came back: I would be permitted to wear trousers only if I wore the uniform skirt over them, like some of the Muslim girls chose to do. I cried.

I was about fourteen at this point, newly diagnosed with an Autism Spectrum Disorder, or ASD. Since autism often involves sensory hypersensitivities, as well as varying degrees of disregard for societal norms and expectations, I attributed my hatred of my school skirt to my ASD and didn't think too hard about it. Similarly, autistic people are often afraid of or otherwise averse to change, so when I had a screaming meltdown about the inevitable growth of my breasts at age twelve, it only seemed logical to attribute my distress to my autism. Battling through puberty and high school as an autistic girl was a herculean task all on its own, and I didn't have the time or the energy or the vocabulary or any of the other resources I would have needed to identify that there was something else going on until I was seventeen.

I first came across the word 'genderfluid' online and hurried to look it up, eager to learn something new about LGBT+ identity (I had come out as bisexual at fourteen, to nobody's real surprise, but I'd stopped all my introspection there – between that and the ASD, I had ample explanation as to why I felt so different from my peers.) The definition was short and without nuance, probably along the lines of 'an individual whose gender identity and self-expression varies between two or more genders.' It surprised me; I'd heard of transgender people, of course, but only those who identified as binary genders. Still, satisfied with this new nugget of information, I clicked away from my web search and returned to whatever I'd been reading.

I continued to struggle with the performance of femininity, and I continued to misattribute that struggle to my autism. I avoided makeup and assumed it was because of the way it felt on my face. I avoided dresses and assumed it was because of the way they moved against my thighs. I avoided perfume and assumed it was because of my sensitivity to strong smells. And, in my mounting resentment towards my assigned sex, I kept returning to one thought: I wish I was genderfluid so I wouldn't have to be a girl all the time.

Not, so I wouldn't have to dress like a girl all the time or so I wouldn't have to wear skirts and makeup or so I wouldn't have to deal with people recommending I make myself look more feminine. My gripe wasn't with the pressures of femininity. It wasn't that I dearly wanted to present as traditionally feminine and was struggling with it. It was that I was, in my own eyes and in others', a girl.

It took me an embarrassingly long time to realise that an abject hatred of your assigned gender might indicate that you don't actually identify with that gender.

There were and are aspects of femininity that I liked and still like. I love eyeliner (providing it's the right texture), I love having my legs out (but prefer shorts to swishy skirts) and, on about 55% of all days, I love my boobs. But I've realised that there are elements of femininity I only want to engage with subversively, and there are days I'd rather be perceived as a twink in drag than as a girl in a dress. All of this is difficult to navigate already, and the difficulty increases manifold when you stir in the autism.

I have very little understanding of how I'm perceived by others because I have very little understanding of how everything is perceived by others. The ability to get 'inside someone's head' and understand how they think, and feel is called cognitive empathy, and I do not have it. Not naturally, at any rate – when I know someone really well and work really hard, I can draw conclusions about what's going on inside their head, but that's a lot of effort to go to when I could just ask. Regarding gender, this is both a blessing and a curse: a blessing because I don't know for certain that people are reading me as female until they refer to me that way, and a curse because I can often present more femininely than I mean to by mistake. You know that quote from Eddie Izzard, when he replied to a question about him wearing women's clothes with, 'They're not women's clothes. They're my clothes. I bought them'? That's how I feel about expressing my nonbinary identity. I don't want my clothes or myself to be read as feminine just because of their shape or colour or whatever else; I just want them to be read as mine.

Navigating the world as a nonbinary autistic person is exhausting. I don't know how to communicate my gender even to the people who would understand it, and I'm all too aware that some people categorically would not. But my autism also gives me a fantastic cushion in that I don't notice people's snide tones or malicious glares when they misgender me, and I allow myself to assume they've simply overlooked my masculinity and/or androgyny rather than that they're actively trying to undermine my identity. It also gives me an extra layer of immunity to societal nonsense about how to 'correctly' perform my gender, since I neither understand nor care about the way that society thinks I should behave.

I wish I'd had the vocabulary to convey to my mum or my school or myself that I was nonbinary when I was fourteen, but more than that I wish I'd had the energy and the self-confidence required to spot that something was out of place. I absorbed the message that I was too sensitive, defectively female and making a fuss about nothing, and I wish I'd been calm enough and stable enough to challenge that. I could have found vocabulary, community, role models and validation if only I hadn't been busy trying to survive adolescence as an autistic person perceived as a girl.

Still, I can make up for the lost time. I now have the resources to offer validation and clarity to other autistic nonbinary people who aren't sure where their sensory issues end and their gender identity begins, I don't need to ask permission to present in a way that makes me feel comfortable, and, most importantly, I have thrown away that wretched school skirt.

Queer Fortune Cookies

By L. Zhu (they/them)
Content warnings: *racism*

I do not like to view the world in binaries; in polar opposites where existence only resides in One or The Other.

At the same time, however, I struggle with the liminality between and among these various plots on the graph - or, rather, where I reside in these liminal spaces.

This anxiety manifests in numerous contexts. As I have grown older and my horizons have expanded to understand new realities of being, my various identities have shifted from what I once knew as a child born in China, adopted by a Caucasian single mother as a baby, and raised in a homogenous town in the Midwest. Traveling to college - including the consequential removal of that limited environment - led to me questioning different parts of myself and discovering new ones.

When people nowadays ask how I realized I was non-binary, I tell them the truth, no matter how vague and unspectacular it may sound: one day I woke up in my bed and realized I wasn't a woman like I had understood myself to be for nineteen years

I think there's a common misconception about non-cis identities where it's believed that signs that hinted at the impending realization since childhood. For me, there was no build up; though I did go through a tomboy stage when I was younger, that was less about not aligning with the conceptions of girl- and womanhood and more about not being interested in femininity (this was, admittedly, with no small amount of internalized misogyny as well). It was not so much a hike to discover this identity but rather an "Oh shit, I'm already at the peak of this mountain" ordeal.

Certainly, I've struggled with different aspects of my gender identity over the past few years, including various brazen but misguided attempts to alter my aesthetic to better 'fit' the prototype of being non-binary (I chopped my near-waist-long hair into a masculine style with an undercut the summer after discovering my identity, and avoided feminine clothing for a couple of years). It took me a while to understand that being non-binary is for no one else's sake but my own and that conception of prototypes for identities can be exclusive and alienating. For some time, I struggled with figuring out what non-binary exactly means to me, but I've mostly come to terms with my uncertainty as of late: I am neither man nor woman, and that's all there really is to it.

What I've found particularly interesting (and, quite frankly, unexpected) about my gender identity journey is how it parallels my struggle to find a racial and ethnic identity that I feel I belong to. As with my gender, I never really contemplated my ethnicity: I was Chinese, and nearly everyone around me was white - friends, peers at schools, those at activities. When I was very young, my mother tried to integrate as much Chinese culture into our household as possible, such as celebrating the Lunar New Year Festival and reading Chinese folklore. But since I had so few Chinese friends or other Chinese figures to interact with, I didn't see the point.

Arriving at a university whose second largest racial composition is Asian was a stark change of pace for me. As I was drawn to Asian spaces on campus, I first began to struggle with the sense of liminality again - sure, I looked Chinese, but I could not speak it and I did

111

not have Asian parents like the vast majority of the other students. I could not understand the popular culture references, never mind the actual words students spoke to one another. In this sense, I was truly Americanized: over the four years of my attendance, I involved myself in many East Asian cultural and language courses and even participated in our production/celebration of the Lunar New Year Festival my senior year, but that sense of Imposter Syndrome never quite dissipated for me.

Again, I found myself suspended in this space of *between*; of Not Quite.

For a long time, this bothered me, and in some ways still does. I am a person who likes to know where they stand in everything - how well I perform at work, how my friendships are faring (are they healthy, do they need more/less time and dedication, etc.), what ways I can improve. I like knowing what I am so I can evaluate my standing and take any subsequent actions/adjustments I deem necessary. Uncertainty leaves me anxious and that's a harsh reality in a world that is somehow both predictable and incredibly unpredictable at the same time.

I remember a friend in high school once called me a twinkie (I have also heard it referred to as a 'banana'): yellow on the outside, white on the inside. At the time, I wasn't offended; I felt like I had *done* it; that I had made it with my peers, and they viewed me as themselves. Acceptance is a basic human need and I felt it there, regardless of how offensive and racist that 'acceptance' was in retrospect.

Now, sometimes, I fear that others (namely, those in the East Asian community) view me as more of a fortune cookie: Chinese-appearing, but actually fabricated in America. Unlike the acceptance I had felt during my first misleading nickname, this perceived label leaves a bitter taste in my mouth and a pang of isolation (maybe even of shame) in my chest. And, in some ways, I don't think I can say I blame them: I have not undergone the same cultural and historical experiences they have undergone, so I often question my right to use the same title as they do.

But just as though I would never negate a queer person's experience because they have not identified as such for as long as another queer person (whether it be in the realm of gender, sexuality, or otherwise/both), I know I should not do the same with my experiences, ethnic or queer. Especially with my bisexuality (I previously identified as aromantic and asexual for a couple of years in college), I sometimes wonder if these are all just somehow easy way outs for me to take; a product of indecisiveness. But none of these aspects of who I am are by choice.

It's taken some time, but I am slowly coming to terms with my existence to find answers in all of these weird spectrums of identity. Especially with gender and sexuality, this has been a fairly daunting task, and I have to accept that I may not arrive at answers for long stretches of time - or that one answer that might make sense now could potentially be discarded for a different answer that makes more sense at a later point in time. No matter how much I may not like it, ambiguity in these spaces is normal, and chances are no one is ever 100% certain of their entire identity.

The last thing I or anyone in a similar position should do is let this ambivalence make us feel shunned from the non-binary or queer community. There are already too many others that don't believe in us; to join them would be the greatest disappointment of all.

And I Swagger

By Artie Carden (they/them)
Content warnings: *misgendering, transphobia, t-slur*

My name is Artie, and I Swagger.

My name is Artie and I am non-binary. I use 'they/them' pronouns. This identity took me a long time to grasp. I am also disabled. I don't like to dance around that word. I am queer and disabled. This is my reality.

A few years ago, I wrote a poem called *Ode To My Binder*. It was about the idea of hating my body for a long time until I figured out my identity and started wearing clothes and things like binders to represent myself. It mentions my mental health struggles and some links to chronic pain, all wound up into a humorous rhyming poem.

I felt good when wearing a binder. I liked how it made me look in clothes and especially in formal wear. I quickly realised wearing it wasn't going to be a regular thing, however. In my early twenties, my chronic pain started to set in. Anything that made it worse, had to go.

I've had Hyper-Mobility my entire life and a few years ago it became Hyper-Mobility Syndrome, which comes with a lot of chronic pain, fatigue, and some regular injuries. A lot of people with HMS dislocate joints, however, I only dislocate two lower ribs on each side. This is the one dislocation no one can really do anything about. I've asked professionals for advice; they had none. Wearing a binder that crushes my main location of injury was kind of impossible.
So, the main thing I had that validated my gender dysphoria, I could no longer wear. I felt like everything I had just found had been taken away again.

I had to learn to be okay with not wearing a binder when I felt like I needed one. My health and comfort are more important. I'd had near panic attacks in bathroom stalls on nights out because I couldn't breathe and struggled to yank it off over my head. I didn't want that to become my normal. My normal had already begun.

Multiple painkillers twice or more a day, testing new ones and being so dizzy I couldn't move without wanting to vomit. Pills for the stomach acid taking so many pills caused. Ibuprofen and sports gels rubbed onto my joints before a long day, desperately trying to avoid popping pills first thing. Chiropractors, Osteopaths, Physiotherapists, Rheumatologists, hydrotherapy, acupuncturists, massage therapists, 'alternative medicines'; I was desperate for something to work. I'm still looking.

I have joint supports on hand, a couple of fold up walking sticks, backup painkillers for my backups. My life is now based around what might possibly happen. I don't have time to feel self-conscious about boobs. So, I stopped caring.

The LGBT+ community is so inaccessible for disabled people; I never meet anyone in my local area. I love to go out clubbing because I really like to dance, but I have to wear earplugs because it's too loud. I have to find a seat to recuperate and those are far and few between. People bump and push me, a lot of clubs only have access by stairs, and let's be honest, it's really expensive to get in anywhere.

Dating is weird. I've had people match with me on dating sites only to tell me I'm a frigid tr*nny and block me. I always wonder if people will respect my pronouns. One lady outside a gay bar that's no longer there was surprised when I introduced myself with my birth name. She said, and I quote, "I thought your name would be Dylan or something," you know, an acceptable unisex name. Can I flirt with gay dudes because I'm not a woman? Will lesbians only see me as a lesbian? I'm openly bisexual for context. A cis man hasn't flirted with me with since I cut my hair four years ago, so should I even bother trying?

I met a lesbian recently; I had been introduced to her with my birth name and 'she/her' pronouns. Both she and this straight girl said they'd call me Artie and use 'they/them' pronouns if I wanted and I bashfully said, "yes, that would be preferable thank you…" Yet, she did not once get them right even when it was just the three of us.

I have a select few friends who have known me for a few years who do their best. I say, 'do their best' because they knew me as something else for years and years. They mess up sometimes, but they correct it. Even though I have one friend who still uses my birth name, we've been friends for 13 years and he said to me recently that I seem more me, and more at ease with myself. I only have two friends who saw me at my absolute worst. Lost, depressed and suicidal. I viciously hated my body. My body now isn't exactly what I wanted, but I've learned my body doesn't have to be anything. My body is mine and I have put it through some shit. Here I am now, I wouldn't say I'm 'happy', but I'm okay. My lows aren't anywhere near as low, my highs are more often and mostly self-made, and I love creating. I love telling my story; I love adding to the growing expanse of work for and by marginalised people. Go to therapy. Even if it's not to talk about your gender, going to therapy is and always will be the best advice I could give anyone.

I've learned to be proud of who I am. I have come a long way on every path. I've wandered these woods a long time and I've finally found a stream and a patch of sunlight.

I want to end this with one of the most iconic quotes I've ever found. Even through all this

'as a cripple, I swagger'
– Nancy Mairs, On Being A Cripple.

Rotten Fruit

By Stephanie (she/her & they/them)
Content warnings: *catcalling, misogyny, assault,*
violence, car accident imagery

Do you remember me?

I'm the femme you catcalled the other day.
The one you stared down crooked like
stitched up clippings from pulp magazines
like I'm still saving up for that decoder ring.

I'm still here.

Like the sting of your mother's pepper spray
the night she was beat up on her way home from work
while you were too busy flipping butterfly knives
through your fingers to recognize your privilege.

Still here, like a mosquito bite. Like a smoker's cough.

Remember me?

I'm every person you've ever lied to,
every bad decision you've ever made
finally catching up to you in the back alley of a biker bar
and smashing open your skull like oncoming traffic.

I'm every other driver on the highway when your brakes
give out.

I'm the oven you left on at home,
The rotten fruit you left out for the flies.

Do you remember me?
I'm the femme you catcalled the other day.
And I remember everything.

Bearing Witness To My Body

By CJ Venable (they/them)
Content warnings: *internalised fatphobia, use of 'sissy'*

My body has been fat longer than it has been nonbinary. As a kid, I remember being forced to wear sweatpants in hideous primary colors because my parents knew I would outgrow any regular pants they might buy for me. For them, it was an economic decision: it was cheaper. In high school, my aesthetic was goth: long black hair, pants with chains and shirts with mesh. I was just as fat, but at least I thought I was cute sometimes. When I was in college, once I could afford to buy my own clothes and build a style all my own, I saw what my parents saw a dozen years before: clothes for fat people are sparse and expensive. My wardrobe was made up of bland jeans that were too long - being a 44"/28" is not easy to shop for - and t-shirts from high school choirs. I could feel that these things were sufficient to cover my body, but they lacked the soul that I knew was buried under all that flesh. Which is not to say my soul is hiding under my fat, but at that time, I might have thought it was. For what felt like forever, I hated my fat body and did everything I could to hide it. And hide from it.

Eventually, I saw myself. I looked, not over, but through. I took an inordinate amount of time during my sophomore year of college truly looking at my body. Was I always curved like that? Maybe it's nice to be soft and supple, rather than firm and unyielding. Would anyone else think my body might be nice to touch, to hold, to love? The conclusion I came to, after months of looking at myself in mirrors, sleeping naked to be reminded of the limits of my body and going beyond them, was that yes, my fat body was beautiful, and lovable, and worthy of lust, and powerful. This smart fat kid had more to offer than just a mind that could never stop thinking.

But even with all that deep contemplation about the parts that were always me, but I wished weren't, I didn't know how to bear witness to my gender. My childhood was full of gender norm subversion - I was always terrible at sports, played with makeup, and had an extensive Polly Pocket collection - but when I came out as queer aged thirteen, I thought that was it. My femme experiences were a reflection of my sissy homo desires. I never thought that my gender, being my mother's son or the middle brother, was up for debate. I was stuck with that M, assigned at birth, but I could camp it up as needed, right? It was something I felt like I couldn't ask too many questions about, and so I didn't. It nagged at me, and I ignored it. For a while.

In graduate school, I had an assignment to research and journal in the voice of a marginalized college student. As a white, queer person, I spent that semester thinking deeply about the experiences, struggles, and power of trans women of color. I felt so uncomfortable the whole time, both for speaking in the voice of a person with multiple marginalizations that I didn't have, but also because it forced me to look inward and think critically about my gender. What about those times when I felt trapped by the idea of 'being a man'? The ways I would ally myself with femmes but feel like I was an imposter and an intrusion into space where I, as a 'man', couldn't belong? I am still not sure if the assignment was a good one, to think I could take on identities like a cloak. But in doing it, the floodgates broke and so did my gender. I fractured the binary that I held within myself and finally acknowledged how my own fat body felt outside of any system of gender that I had ever seen or understood. I wept at the realization that I had been holding together for so long this thing inside me that I never even wanted. I had spent more energy than I even realized on holding back the things that would be too femme, too camp, too queer for those around me to handle. For me to handle.

From that moment, I have identified myself as a fat, queer and genderqueer person. Those three things are bound up with duct tape and string. All the images I have ever had of nonbinary people have been thin, androgynous people who can wear oversized shirts and tight pants and ride their longboards into the sunset. I knew I would never look like that, and so again I wept for a body that I had only recently come to love and hold with care. I have had to stumble forward, finding ways to make my fat body feel and look the way I want it to. Sometimes I just give up on the idea that people will ever see me as nonbinary. No matter how many times I introduce myself with my pronouns or correct people when they try to group me with men, it seems like all people will ever see is what they want to see. It can be hard to hold all three together.

I remember being mistaken for a woman once as a young teenager, my round body and breasts looking feminine enough, until I turned my head and my patchy facial hair caused the person to take back their statement in a fit of embarrassment. Now, I wear a full beard, probably the largest source of confusion when I tell people that I'm not a man. If I was going to queer my gender, my beard was going with me. My size makes people think of me as imposing and powerful; 'did you play football in high school?' is a common refrain. But I see myself as soft, my curves flowing gently over my frame. Only in the last few years have I been able to find clothes that are cut for my body and flow in ways that suggest the fullness of my gender complexity. Slowly but surely, I'm finally eliminating the polo shirts and boring slacks from my closet. I could have done that years ago if I weighed a hundred pounds less than I do.

Every space I enter, the physical body I inhabit is on my mind. Will I have a comfortable place to sit that fits my fat body? Am I safe to wear nail polish and jewelry that helps me express my gender? Will I be ignored or erased, even as more people use things like introductions with pronouns as a non-performative display of inclusion? I am also constantly aware of the other kinds of considerations that nonbinary people of color must attend to that I as a white person do not. These material consequences from the material of my body cannot be separated from the socially constructed interiority of my identities.

This essay is my testimony as a fat nonbinary genderqueer person, a testimony of how the body that carries me is also something that I carry with me. My weight is a weight that I feel in my soul. Sometimes that is a buoyant joy, lifting up the myriad possibilities I know are inside me. Other times it is a heavy reminder of what many see when they look at me: a fat dude in floral pants. But this weight always grounds me, holds me to the Earth, and reminds me of what I am: whole.

Fig. 10 by Eireni Moutoussi (they/them)

Reach

By Leo Middlebrook (he/him & they/them)

I slowly unbutton to bare my chest
in all its softness and nearly without shame.
Fingers stiff with disuse I reach
to loosen the band that encircles my ribs

Maybe today I will finally breathe
if my lungs still remember the motion,
If my breasts don't sit heavy, imposing
a weight I don't care to bear.

To walk unseen and freely
to lie exposed, outside the bounds
The lines in the sand dissolve with the seafoam and
soon
I forget they were ever there at all

I loosen the band that encircles my ribs
but the steel leaves its mark on my skin.
Are the bonds ones I wrought and if not,
is it too much to hope for release?

The comfort of shadows may be one I've outgrown
reaching instead, arms outstretched, to be known

To be seen and breathe freely
in all my softness
without shame.

Here Are My Pieces

By Avi Burton (he/him & they/them)

To use the cliché -

I want to shed my skin like a chrysalis
and leave this bloody form behind.
Not to become a butterfly;
but because this cocoon is not safe.
Milk-white, it used to hold me -
that was good. I needed it, to
contain the flesh that grows,
tumor-like in places that I do not want.
I built a new spirit and outgrew my skin.
Now it chokes me, thin strands pulling
and fraying me to pieces. (Here are my pieces:
lips. breasts. vagina). know this temple is not meant for
me.
(I know I am jigsaw pieces that do not fit - another
cliché)
and now my cocoon only reminds
me of what I am not. Its embrace
is a chokehold.
It used to bind me,
and now it strangles.

And That's Okay

By Rhian Beam (they/them & he/him)

I visualize myself and I see someone that's not me, in
the mirror.
I see masculine features, deeper voice.
I see rounded curves, and pink all over my limbs,
my legs hairy, and my heart a feminine pile of glitter.

Fig. 11 by Rae Allison-Stork (they/them)

And that's okay.
I have always been in between or not at all
and I'm not being nuanced, and there's no 'deeper
meaning'.
I simply feel in between, or all genders at once

and sometimes even none, it is void.
It can depend on the hour, the day, the week.
I thrive in the liminal construct.
There are two hallways, and I walk through the wall
between them
and that's okay.
I feel I am not real.
I feel I am a radical being that isn't human.
But what is true? I am human.
I deserve that respect; I deserve that right.
I am not radical, I am normal.
I am nonbinary.
And that's okay.

My Backwards Gender Journey

By Peter Gillet (he/him)

Content warnings: surgery mention, suicide mention

I would like to preface this essay by saying everyone's gender journey is valid. I also need to say that if someone needs surgery to live their best life, then they should get that surgery.

Over the years, I have listened to many life stories, and have followed the lives of my transgender friends. As I continue my journey to living authentically as a non-binary person, I have realized much of the sequence of my own experiences seems backwards to theirs. I hope my story serves to widen the understanding of the human condition, promote genuine respect for gender diversity, and increase acceptance of these differences.

I'll start at the beginning and the catalyst for my gender journey. I was most likely born and living as a cisgender boy until around the age of 10 or 11. At that time, based upon the history of my symptoms, an adenoma (non-cancerous tumour) started growing on my pituitary gland. Being the master gland, if it doesn't directly control something, it controls the gland which does. In my case, the adenoma produced prolactin and lots of it. This is the hormone which allows mammals to produce milk.

In hindsight, and with the reading I've been doing on transgender issues, the adenoma essentially acted as a crude puberty blocker. Through my teens and early twenties, the level of my sexual attraction to others wavered between asexual and greysexual. I had no interest in masturbation. I still haven't experienced an orgasm. My body stopped developing towards manhood

129

and started veering towards motherhood. It found a path somewhere between the two. As you can imagine, my chest became larger and softer (gynecomastia), but not enough to be an obvious sign of a medical condition. It didn't occur to me to mention my lack of sex drive to a doctor. I just knew it as being my life, and not as a symptom that something else might be happening.

While my body was taking its own path, so too was my gender identity being transformed by the constant flood of hormones. While I consciously thought of myself as a man, that surface belief was increasingly at odds with my developing gender identity. Through my twenties, I constantly struggled with my masculinity or rather my lack thereof. I grew nurturing, to an almost self-destructive level. I didn't understand the psychological turmoil going on within me. Even when another trauma led me to see a psychiatrist, none of these sexual issues led to any medical follow-up. While I was able to work through the trauma, the gender dysphoria I was experiencing remained undiagnosed.

After meeting and falling in love with a beautiful woman, we agreed to get married. My low sex drive and lack of orgasms became a more pressing issue, but again the medical community treated the symptoms rather than looking for a root cause. After a couple of years of having trouble conceiving a child, we were referred to specialists. A simple hormone blood test revealed the cause. At the age of thirty-one, I had five times the average prolactin level of a lactating parent. It was slowly killing me and had to be removed.

Brain surgery removed most of the adenoma, but I was prescribed cabergoline, indefinitely, to suppress the remaining prolactin-producing cells. I also started HRT because my body would not produce testosterone. I was thankful for the relatively easy and good results of the surgery. However, the explanation for why I was different only served to increase my gender dysphoria. Perhaps it was due to living in a relatively rural part of Canada, but none of the medical professionals I met ever mentioned the possibility of being transgender, or of suffering from gender dysphoria.

I continued this way for over a dozen years, and it was hell. Due to the undiagnosed dysphoria, I struggled with suicidal thoughts. I obsessed about having surgeries to reduce the feminine aspects of my body and "fix" the less masculine parts. I had no idea how we could afford such voluntary procedures, and I felt selfish for wanting them.

Five years ago, I met one of my closest friends. He and I confided many things in one another, and one day he told me he was transgender. He hadn't started transitioning yet, so I felt extremely honoured with this confidence. Of course, I wanted to be a better friend for him, so that is when I started researching transgender topics. At the time, I was still unaware of non-binary genders.

One evening, almost two years ago, I was reading a website about non-binary genders and intersex people. I paused, considered my medical history, and asked myself aloud, "what if I'm not a man?" That was the first time I experienced gender euphoria. It felt like something finally stopped struggling within me. I no longer saw my body as being flawed and needing to be changed. I no longer thought of myself as a man. My depression has been easily managed since that very moment. It took more research to eliminate some of the genders I might or might not be, and I have settled on the umbrella term of non-binary.

As you can see, my path started with a physical transition, decades of dysphoria and HRT, and only then realizing my gender identity no longer matched what was assigned at birth. The pathology which initiated this sequence in no way means there is anything wrong with my current gender. I am not upset that the adenoma took so long to be discovered, as surgical and pharmaceutical remedies greatly improved over those twenty years. Gender theory also significantly expanded over those decades, as did awareness of it outside of academia. It took time for me to meet and befriend the people who could introduce me to those ideas. I no longer see these troubles in my past as a burden, but as a toolbox labelled "to help others". I want the paths of others to be clearer, and easier to follow than mine was.

From here my path will be more typical. I am now socially transitioning, and I am looking forward to legally transitioning. I am happy to tell my story, and I am eager to amplify the voices of other non-binary and transgender people. I challenge binary options for gender at work and elsewhere. For example, I am the first author to be registered as non-binary instead of male or female in my province's library system. Of course, I am still learning and will be for the rest of my life.

I'm Full Of Drains And Tubes And I'm Happy

By Aviel McDermott (they/them & he/him)
Content warnings: *surgery mention, transphobia*

Sometimes you gotta peel away
the bullshit with a knife.
Feel the scars and raw skin,
your pulse on the surface.
Bleed, and hurt, and risk it all
To find yourself bruised and swollen,
and ugly in everyone else's eyes,
Just to take a breath of fresh air
and live your own life.

My body is nonbinary and now
it's visibly so. I like it, even
if I never had a choice on the scars,
but it also scares me.
My body is transgender and now
it's visibly so. I love it, even
if it truly scares me
because I am not alone.

I wake up now in the mornings
and smile at the scar running
all the way across my flat chest.
I always thought I'd make a
very pretty boy and a very butch woman.

I have been told, again and again,
that transitioning is from man to woman

or woman to man. Like it was only ever
one path. Like that isn't a dull simplification
of what it means. As if major surgery
couldn't count as transition unless
I follow all the steps
Someone else laid out for me.

Transgender, nonbinary: they're one
and the same for me.
My nonbinary identity is transgender
and my transition is nonbinary.

Removing my breasts didn't mean
removing my chest: it meant revealing it.
I was scared going in, and coming out,
and even now weeks after
I still feel my scars every day.
I have so much life to live!
I never liked taking risks like this but
I have so much life to live.
I just take a breath of fresh air
and live my own life.

Gender Euphoria

By J.J. Hamilton (Any Pronouns)

The first instance
that comes to mind
is the time we went
to karaoke,
and I wore
my hair in a braid
topped with a beanie,
a loose tank top
with a strappy
bralette
underneath,
black skinny jeans,
and purple Converse.
And they said to me,
"You look really
Nonbinary tonight."
But it's also every
time I use an
all gender bathroom.
It's every time I shave my head.
It's every time my boyfriend
says that the song Rebel, Rebel
reminds him of me.
It's the euphoria
that comes from
a lack of gender.
It's unique, and it's beautiful.

Fig. 12 by Caleris (they/them)

Dysphoria As Malware

By J.M. Cottle (he/him)

*Content warnings: dysphoria, surgery mention,
internalised transphobia*

If you could get a flat chest by waving a wand, with no
pain or risk of complications, would you do it? If you
could get a flat chest without telling a single person
about it, would you do it? If you were the only person left
in the world, would you still want it?

For me, answering "yes" to these questions led
me to the operating table for a double mastectomy, also
known as top surgery. After years of wild swings
between "give it to me yesterday" and "I could never do
that," I made my decision because I was exhausted.
Uncertainty takes a lot out of you. In the end, I knew
"no" wasn't a definitive enough answer because I could
always return to the question. So, at last, I removed the
temptation.

My uncertainty wasn't because I didn't know if I
wanted a flat chest - I definitely wanted a flat chest. I just
wasn't sure that I needed one, and if I didn't need it, why
put myself through surgery? If I didn't need it, did I even
deserve it? Having survived for so long with this body, I
thought I was being ridiculous to want to take such a
drastic step. For what? I wasn't suicidal, or even truly
miserable. I was just inconvenienced. Maybe I should
take the advice given to cisgender people and learn to
love my body rather than carve off pieces of it.

After surgery, after the pain was gone and my
range of movement returned, I felt... normal. *What?*
Normal? I had never felt normal before in my life.

When I requested a letter from a therapist
recommending top surgery, I described my dysphoria as

disappointment. I told her that when I saw a picture of myself or caught a glimpse of my reflection, there was a prick of confusion. What was wrong with my chest? Oh... right. Nothing. It was supposed to stick out like that. And then I was disappointed because I didn't really look the way my mind believed that I looked. This wasn't what I thought dysphoria should feel like, but the therapist was convinced.

After surgery, a thick layer of static in my thoughts was abruptly gone. Without realizing it, I used to keep my chest always in my mind. Now I could jump, slump, bend over, do push-ups, or hug someone without worrying about what my chest was doing. It was like surgery had deleted a computer virus that was sucking up my processing power, and now I could function a lot more smoothly. I had gotten so used to that constant, low-level anxiety and stress that I thought it was part of my personality. In fact, it was only dysphoria.

I didn't just deserve top surgery - I needed it, although I didn't realize that until after it was done. And I started to wonder - what if I had more gender-related malware on my hard drive? What if more and more of my anxiety could be deleted?

I'm genderless, but the only doctor I told about my lack of gender was the therapist. I let the surgeon and all the nurses believe I was a man, for convenience, and they were happy and excited for me. They called me "he," congratulated me on my manly attributes, and encouraged me to continue along the female-to-male path prescribed by my insurance. I felt like I was playing a part for them. It was odd but enjoyable. I used to think that being taken as a man would bother me as much as being taken as a woman, but that wasn't the case. It didn't feel like me, but it felt good.

Of course, it felt good. For once in my life, other people - people in power - were convinced I was doing exactly the right thing when it came to my gender. They were celebrating me. It was tantalizing. Maybe I could pursue this. Maybe I could take testosterone, change to "he" pronouns, become a man.

It's clear to me that this is the correct wording. Become a man. For most trans men, this is a gross misunderstanding of their situation because they've always been men, and their transition is only changing their physical and social selves. That isn't the case for me. I've always been genderless. If I become a man, it's going to be a change, a departure, a conscious choice to alter my internal identity.

The decision to take testosterone was just as difficult as the decision to have top surgery. Testosterone isn't as sudden or painful, but its discomforts last longer and its effects are not as private. No one noticed my flat chest, but a cracking voice and a fuzzy mustache are very public.

If you could get facial hair and a deeper voice without telling a single person about it, would you do it? Yes, but that isn't an option. I applied my first dose of testosterone gel on September 23, 2015. After five minutes of pacing and hyperventilating, I washed it off.

The next day I began my testosterone therapy in earnest because I knew that if I didn't, the uncertainty would always haunt me. Three years later I can't remember the last time a stranger read me as a woman, and my mask of manliness has melded into my being, becoming part of me. It's comfortable enough that sometimes, I forget that I'm not actually a man. I didn't have the same sudden clarity that came with top surgery, but every new change - smaller hips, bigger shoulders, a thicker neck, being called "sir" and "son" and "brother" - removed another layer of noise.

Changing my physical self and my social self didn't have to change my identity, but I think it might have. I still call myself genderless if asked by someone in the LGBTQ community, but I'm no longer sure that's the truth. I live my life as a man. I enjoy it. When someone makes a comment about men, I feel like I'm included. For better or worse.

Is there a difference between feeling comfortable living as a man, and being a man? I was deeply uncomfortable living as a woman, but I was also deeply uncomfortable living as a genderless person. Society made it so. The anxiety and stress of pushing away all gendered things, of expecting misgendering around every corner, was barely distinguishable from the dysphoria of living as the wrong gender. It was a different kind of malware, but the effects were the same. The computer still didn't run properly. Now it does.

Maybe I'm pretending to be a man because it's easier that way. If I am, can you blame me? If you were the only person left in the world, would your gender be any different? Does it matter?

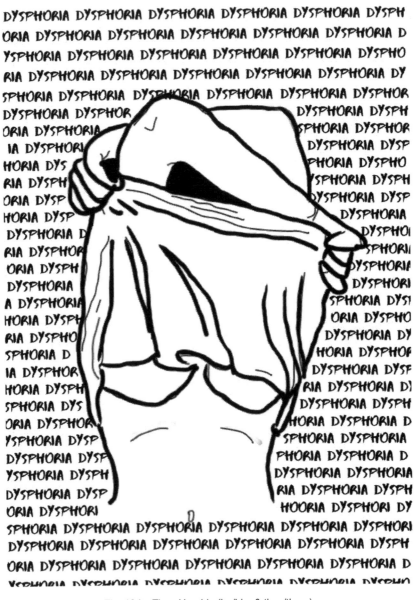

Fig. 13 by Theo Hendrie (he/him & they/them)

140

One Day

By Olive Dakota (they/them)

One day.
One day you will be out.
One day you will get
your first dose of estrogen;
your first "they" from a stranger;
your first dress or skirt or
whatever the hell you want to wear.
It's your life, why don't you act like it?
Take some initiative.
Fuck what they say - you are
you
and you are
beautiful, and loved,
so so loved.
You will always be loved.
You will always be you.

Wrong With Me

By David Caggiano (he/him & it/its)
Content warning: *internalised transphobia*

I am somebody else.
I'm not myself anymore.
I left that face behind me.
Don't remind me of the girl

who used to comb her hair
and stare at her reflection
in the mirror. She'd stop and
whisper to herself
"Why don't you look familiar?"

What is wrong with me?
So many years of tears I cried that dried
on cheeks that weren't mine.
So many pictures taken of fake smiles painted
on to hide the hurt inside.

So many nights I'd lie in bed
trapped and lost inside my head,
and wonder why, wonder why,
wonder why don't I look familiar?

What is wrong with me?
I know what's wrong with me.
Wanna know what's wrong with me?
Absolutely nothing.

The Beard As A Symbol Of Femininity

By Red Fawkes (ze/zer)

because
I mean:
how could it not
be?
what could be more feminine
than growing back
despite all that has tried to cut
you down?

Fig. 14 by Ab Brooks (they/them)

Dangling

By Lu "Ship" Everman (they/them)
Content warnings: self-harm, pregnancy, eating
disorders, transphobia

Those wide hips beneath my palms arrived uninvited.
There was no binding able to hide them, no disguising
their curves even beneath the most shapeless of pants
or the baggiest of shirts. When I entered a room, I was
overwhelmed by the eyes that I imagined were drawn to
my permanently altered bones and the ligaments that
betrayed me. Before my baby hollowed out a place for
himself in my muscles, I could ignore the itching
beneath my skin.

After, I couldn't find enough fingers to scratch.
The classical femininity of my nude form attacked me
from every mirror, forcing me to stare at my one forever
oversized breast; the saucers of my too-brown nipples;
my new full belly patchworked with stretch marks. I had
been an "androgynous girl" once, as the father of my
child called me. Those new measuring tape-defying
curves knew androgyny was no longer mine to have.

Ten months prior, I would have frowned at my
reflection and forgotten to eat for a few days until the
image changed and I found myself more pleasing, my
coping mechanism since puberty. I couldn't control my
shape, but I could contain myself, make sure I took up
as little space as possible, coax my waistline to expand
and retract in broken clockwork.

In the days and weeks and months after
delivering my son, however, I felt nothing but sick when I
looked at my own face. I thought it would pass, thought I
would grow accustomed to the changes, thought I could

walk and starve and vomit it away, or else read enough books to fill my head with something else to think about.

Not even Lucille Clifton could make me appreciate those hips of mine. If she couldn't, there was no hope for me. I certainly couldn't do it on my own.

My child's first birthday comes and goes, and I wonder at the why of my womanhood.

Ignoring your gender is easy when you don't have a name for it.

Shopping for my first training bra - accompanied by my mother, aunt, and grandmother like some odd initiation rite, a parade of kin chromosomes passing through the menstrual hut of J.C. Penney - that had been mortifying, but I chalked the feeling up to the absurdity of the situation. I'd spent several months prior hunched over, disguising my developing breasts, doing my best to ignore how wrong my chest looked and the inevitable congratulations on becoming a woman.

This is how everyone feels. It was a comfortable assumption, that all girls were as horrified as I was when I looked in the mirror. The fear was a natural consequence of puberty; we were supposed to hate it just as much as our pimples. We all wanted to take knives to our chests and liberate ourselves.

I let others confine me - girls do that, too, I reminded myself. When a boyfriend in high school told me, "You have the most perfect boobs," I wore my sweaters tighter.

"Don't wear a white bra under a white shirt," my father warned, his face turned away as I leaned against the shopping cart. I nodded at his wisdom and hid my nipples behind beige.
"Adjust your cups like this," my mother said in the fitting room, showing me how to bend over and settle my

breasts above the corset's underwire to support them properly.

This is how everyone feels.

And then, a decade later, I watched my body change as a fetus kicked me into a pregnant shape. Other expectant mothers griped along with me about how uncomfortable we were, about slowly forgetting what our toes looked like. Strangers marveled at how my skin glowed, and suddenly the growing bump was no longer annoying. It was intolerable.

I felt like a real woman, and the knowledge ached more than my curved spine, rivaled my morning sickness. True femininity at last, and it was unbearably hideous.

By degrees, week to week, with every progress photo I shared, all the sickening reminders of this fragile shell began to hurt more and more. I was meant to call it home, except I didn't, I couldn't, because I looked so different in my head with my flat chest and close-cropped hair, toes gripped in wet sand beside the ocean, standing proud in swimming trunks.

I realized this isn't how everyone feels, and I had no idea what to do with the epiphany.

My son nestled against the chest I hated, curled into me as he nursed, gentle sucks of hungry greed. At least my breasts served a purpose. Seeing them as a source of nutrition soothed the growing dysphoria, and I clung to breastfeeding, even when it wasn't working. Especially then, and often to my child's detriment. If I gave him formula, I had failed, and years of bearing a front-loaded burden would become meaningless.

We made it for eighteen months. I still watch him sometimes and wonder if my coping mechanism ever slowed his development and left him starving.

Pundits make jokes about nonbinary terms - Tumblr genders, they call them. Some binary folks, both cis and trans, deem us 'transtrenders'. It's all in our heads; we've gaslighted ourselves; we need to pick a side, stick with it, and give ourselves a normal pronoun.

'They' and 'them' and 'theirs' have been mine since the day I learned what a pronoun was. My English classes formed the first stepping stone of self-actualization, even though I wasn't yet aware there was another path to walk.

An adult now, I scoured the queerer sides of the internet as my child dozed, discovering dozens of new words and terms, finding two that finally clicked. Nonbinary. Transmasculine. Me.

But the binary still applied offline. A server greeted our table - " How are you ladies doing tonight?" and "Have you ladies decided what to order? - and I recoiled. I was out to this circle of cis female friends; I was accepted and loved. Transmasculine. Nonbinary. All of me, with my dangly round-disc earrings that I never wore again, desperate to not look so much like a girl.

When I met with a therapist a few months later, decked in flannel and men's jeans with a practiced gait and resting face to match, she asked if I was transgender or butch.

On Twitter, I talked about wanting HRT, but did I? Would facial hair and a deeper voice make me happy? How could I identify as masculine if I don't look like a man? Why did the word lady bother me, but not the term ma'am?

I constantly questioned myself, yearned for the earrings I put away, rubbed the piercings to make sure they were still there. Just in case. Just because.

My binder traps the chest that needs re-sculpting and the sagged pregnant fat of my abdomen I want carved away. I imagine having the red-scarred lines of those same surgeries tattooed over, my body mine once more claimed and unbroken. It's taken years, but I can dream of standing in the salt-blessed waves in a flowing skirt, skin unshaven, a packer in my boxer briefs, a presentation of every gender I am not.

I can't change my hips. They'll always remind me of the sex I was assigned without consultation and my transformation from maiden to mother. I am transmasculine nonbinary, but I wear scarves and fitted clothes and refuse to contour my face with makeup.

The world will always see me as a woman, no matter what I do. There will never be a time where I walk through life not having to pick and choose which microaggressions hurt most. I will carry the weight of friends who remain steadfast with others who question my gender in private. Burdens cannot be set down; my guard can never be lowered; questions won't disappear, neither mine nor the critics.

But I can look in the mirror again.

Things I Seldom Said

By Dr. Alexandra "Xan" C.H. Nowakowski
(they/them)

When some boy
told me I kissed
like a man
I told him
well at least
that makes
one of us.

Then he passed
me over
for a girl
I took no interest
in being
and later
for a boy
I felt no interest
in becoming.

There were many
like this
after that one
kiss that gave
voice to all those
things I seldom said
in words.

I proposed
to this girl
but also this boy
on a fishing pier

between day and night
was someones then
they and them
and me.

When I said I do
that second time
I kissed them
endlessly
for better
for worse
until the very end
until we fade
into the sea.

What To Wear To Bed

By Melissa Welter (ze/zir)
Content warnings: sexual activity

At fifteen, I am hanging out in a parking lot with a bunch of other queer kids. We're discussing gender roles, waiting to go get dinner together.

"Melissa's a femme," someone says.

I wrinkle my nose. I definitely don't think of myself that way. "I'm not a femme," I protest.

"You wear skirts and dresses."

I look down dubiously at my jeans and t-shirt, typical of the clothes I wear. "Sometimes," I agree.

"Well, then."

Well, what? I want to ask. Apparently, that was it. Dresses equal no admittance to the butch club. My fate is decided. I don't like the dismissive finality of it. I want to make decisions like this for myself, not have other people decide what I am.

I almost say something, but don't.

We are supposed to look nice. We are going out together, somewhere more formal than usual. Everyone needs to dress up. That means, it is explained to us, blouses and long skirts for the girls and slacks and collared shirts for the boys.

I don't want to wear a skirt. I don't want it to the point of incoherent sobbing that won't stop for half an hour. I feel like something core to me is being ripped out. I can't explain what is wrong.

They let me wear pants.

I'm seventeen, the summer before college, and my sweetheart is beautiful. She looks at me with desire and

151

curiosity. I wear daringly short skirts and plunging necklines, the velvet of the dress somehow making me feel safe in it. I wear corduroy pants and button-down shirts. She touches me just the same in both of them. I fall a little bit in love.

Away at a pagan women's camp by myself for the first time that summer, I crush on a butch a little younger than me. I notice my voice pitching high, how I giggle more often and am suddenly more helpless. I see the fleeting eyes of older women, their glances seeming to bestow approval on me. I carry myself differently. I experience how desire can change me.

I date a classmate. She cross-dresses for theatrical purposes.

"Why is it that a man cross-dressing as a woman is instantly funny, whereas a woman cross-dressing as a man has to work so hard at it?" she complains one evening. We are strolling across campus holding hands.

I've been taking a feminist art class. I know the answer to this question. "A man pretending, he would give us his privilege is ludicrous. The idea is funny. A woman pretending to take on the power and authority of a man is threatening."

"Huh," she says, "I never thought of it that way."

Last quarter, I took a class where we explored the intersections of theater and gender. I had never realized the degree to which my socialization as a woman influenced the little ways I interacted with people. I ducked my head, I lowered my eyes, I smiled in borderline flirtation when I wanted to flatter someone.

"Yeah," I say, "it sucks."

In my twenties, all my dress up clothes are 'girl' clothes. I have swirling, floor-length hippy skirts and peasant

152

blouses for ritual. I love the way they move around me when I dance, bare feet pounding the floor. The graceful swoops outline, then conceal, never letting more than a glimpse of my body through. I still draw admiring looks. It is easier when I am dancing; a body in motion is entirely mine.

I try to dance for lovers a few times. In a circle of drums, I turn and stomp and leap. My girlfriend does the same, but she is in her own universe. We aren't orbiting each other. In a field, listening to music blast through speakers, I put my hands on a beautiful woman's hips. I feel electric and aroused. Somehow, I can't make that energy sync. Eventually, I learn to dance only for myself.

I sheathe myself in that feeling at a sky-clad ritual. I've been told these things aren't sexual, that no one is looking "like that". Nerves still coil in my stomach. I begin to dance, letting the rhythm wipe out anything else. I spend the rest of the weekend receiving awkward, leering compliments on how I look while dancing from complete strangers. It is the first time I have felt unsafe in my skin around others. I want to curl up and cover myself, to hide so that no one can see me. I take to wrapping my cloak completely around me and putting the hood up.

I learn what it is like to move at play parties. I wear a little black dress, a leather miniskirt, faux leather pants, or nothing at all. No one touches me. Most people look at my face, regardless of what or how little I am wearing. It's refreshing. Slowly, I learn to trust again, to feel safe in my skin. It is better than the occasional clubbing I have tried.

When I am with a partner, sometimes people's eyes slide right off me, like I have invoked a spell of invisibility. With the right body language, sometimes strangers will cut themselves off mid-sentence and go elsewhere. I love it.

On my own, I go prowling. I learn to look for and express subtler signs of desire than the sliminess that is often present outside. I learn to ask for what I want, and to be graceful even if the answer is "no." Amidst raunchiness and such wide-ranging tastes, it feels safer to explore.

There are possibilities open in these spaces that are closed elsewhere. I ask to be kissed, but nothing else. I ask to touch, but not be touched. I begin to ask for, and receive, different gender markers. Words become part of what I take with me to bed. Each experience, I get to negotiate anew what will be touched, and how.

"You have such beautiful breasts," one partner tells me.

"Mm," I respond. I suppose I do. I let him play with them. My pleasure feels distant. I wish vaguely that he would move on. Eventually, he does.

As time goes on, I take my breasts off the menu more and more often. I can't figure out what to wear anymore, how to show off my body and indicate availability while keeping my breasts under wrap.

Squatting naked on the floor, I gaze into the mirror. Sometimes, it is kind. My body looks like mine, a little hairy, a little soft. When I run my hands over my skin, everything feels like it belongs to me. The me in the mirror seems reflective.

Sometimes, the mirror is not so kind. I poke at the blobs of flesh on my chest. What are these for? I have no children, no plans to nurse a living being. The lumps jiggle when I poke. They refuse to be flattened, oozing out the sides of my covering hands. I frown at myself, unhappy. What am I supposed to do with these awkward parts in the meantime, until the kind days come back?

I suppose it could be worse.

My trans lover dresses me up in my late twenties. We go shopping for boy clothes, something I have been both wistful and timid about. She has a good eye for it. In piles of garage sale items, she pulls out shirts and jeans, holding them up to me. Some she discards. Others, she has me try on. She examines collar sizes and the way my shoulders fit into garments. Under neat layers of buttons, my breasts disappear. The emphasis changes. I square my shoulders and lift my chin.

All my life, I've been told I must display my breasts to be sexy. My girlfriend reaches over and straightens my collar. She steps back and gives me a long, approving look that simmers with desire. I feel a spark. Heat? Hope?

I lick my lips and watch her eyes catch on my mouth. Both, I decide. I gaze back at her.

I should feel more at home here. This party is for trans and nonbinary folks, people like me. The bodies are certainly beautiful to look at. A few people are costumed outrageously or deliciously. Looking at a corset over a flat chest, lace garters and a thong cradling a cock, I feel shy in my towel.

There's a steam room here. I normally love this sort of thing, the soaking heat of it sinking into my bones. I close my eyes and try to enjoy. Naked to my skin, though, I feel odd. Dysphoric. I know the word, now, know what this feeling creeping over me is. Sitting with bodies that bear their difference on the outside, my body looks disappointingly uncomplicated. It doesn't match the way I feel at all.

I try to tell myself that trans people would definitely get this feeling if I spoke up about it. Probably several people are wishing their bodies looked different, too, maybe even wishing their bodies looked something like mine. No one is judging gender by appearance tonight. Still, I stay hesitant, my towel draped over my lap.

I eye the contents of my closet. Sexy, I know. I want to feel sexy at Trans March. What does that mean these days, though? My hands skim over my little black dress, linger on the leather miniskirt. Maybe? With the right top? I touch my collection of button downs. Not stripes. Black over a black skirt makes me look too much like I'm headed to a dungeon.

It'll be cold, I think. Fog sweeps in around the time we march in San Francisco. Pants. Jeans, the tight pair that shows off my ass. Button downs will look oddly formal with that, though. An undershirt, the kind I see guys on the block wearing all the time. White. I frown at the curve of my breasts under it. I add a necklace, a simple heart charm with my girlfriend's name on it. This, too, is like the boys around here. That's better, but still not quite it. I put my grey hat on my head and pull on the brim to situate it.

Ah. I touch the warm brown of my leather jacket. I've tried black ones over the years, but I always gravitate back to this. My dad gave me this jacket. The lining is straight out of the seventies, and it smells faintly like smoke. I slide it on. There. Now, my breasts are hidden. I widen my stance, tilt my chin. Good.

On the train, someone calls me "sir." I smile. My body feels alive.

"Oh." My voice comes out soft, surprised.

My lover looks up at me, lips wrapped around the tip of my cock. She sinks down and backs up, slowly. We have never done this before. As much as I love fucking her, this is something different. It feels selfish, like this pleasure is all for me. And so, so good.

"Oh," I say again, "fuck."

She pulls off for a moment. "Do you like that, baby?"

Fig. 15 by Aiden GD Moore (he/him)

"Yeah." I am breathless.

I strain, more turned on by the second. My body feels right like this, my cunt still there but a cock rising hard between my thighs. My breasts are unimportant, out of reach. My lovers now, in any case, are more careful with my body. After a while, I am desperate. A quick loosening of a strap gives access to my flesh. It takes barely more than a touch to my aching cunt before I am coming.

My lover smiles, smug and delighted. "We definitely should do that again."

157

"Yeah," I agree, shaky.

"Come here," she says, holding out her arms. I crawl into her lap and close my eyes.

On the good days, I wear clothes close to my skin. The curves and folds of my body delight me. I am calm and content. Or, better, I am blazingly confident, meeting the eyes of strangers with a bold smirk. If they mistake me, mistake, who and what I am, that is not my problem. I am wholly genderqueer, whatever I choose to wear.

On the hard days, I wear loose shirts or covering button-downs, erasing any hint of what lies beneath. I cock my chin and straighten up with determination. I have as much right to conceal as to reveal. What I choose to share is no one else's business. I meet any challengers head-on. If I don't precisely feel sexy on those days, I at least feel sharp and put-together.

Dysphoria comes and goes. Out and about, I am careful with myself. I mix signifiers, pairing men's shirts and skirts, boots and jeans with heavy eyeliner, or a dress with a tie. This combination makes my body safe ground, a place where my identity can rest. It chases the sense of disconnect away. I can attract the sort of attention I want. Romping in private with lovers, I dress up or down as it pleases us both. I know I am being seen.

It isn't always easy, but I wear what I want to bed.

The Seams

By Theo Hendrie (he/him & they/them)
Content warnings: *sexual activity*

We strain at the seams of our bodies
with every breath, tugging out the
stitches to see what lies beneath.
Look! What a mess you've made of me.

Embroider my skin, show me how you
see me as more than the sum of my
pieces. Unpick the stitches that form
'girl' to sew me something new.
Groan my name like you know.
Like you see who I really am.

It feels like we were made to do this.
Made to figure out all the ways
we can sew ourselves together
and all the different uses for
hips and hands, tongues and teeth,
lips and the tips of fingers.

So, let me come undone.

The Art Of Gender Performance

By Espi Kvit (they/them)
Content warnings: *sexual activity, misgendering*

Sex work is performance art. It is where the lines between fantasy and reality collide. While I bring myself and my interests into my work, the Espi that appears in one of my pornographic videos is not the Espi that lounges at home covered in blankets in their PJs (which is precisely how I am sitting right now). The Espi that appears in my sex work is the cis, the heteronormative, the easy to swallow (for the most part). The Espi that appears in the real world is the queer, the unusual, the complex. Navigating my gender as a sex worker has added a layer of complexity that I was, admittedly, ill-prepared to deal with when I came out. Between coming to terms with my gender, announcing it to everyone in my life, including my clientele, and learning how to reposition myself as a nonbinary sex worker, the path to where I am now has not been an easy one, and it is a path I still tread through with uneven footing every day.

Coming to terms with my gender was a long and painful process. From a young age, I never felt I fit in with the "feminine." I wonder how normal it is for children to constantly reassure themselves that they like being called "girl." That they love "she" pronouns. That being called "her" is something to be proud of and wear like a badge of honor and any distaste for it would be shameful to all womankind. I went through periods where I started letting my true identity claw its way out, especially between the ages of twelve to fifteen. I was unashamed of looking masculine, acting masculine, sounding masculine. But then the years of being told I needed to be "more feminine" began to finally take hold of me. My junior year of high school, I caved. I began to dress more feminine, act more feminine, sound more feminine. In turn, I was given the validation I had so desired. My mother told me how happy she was that I was finally "acting like a girl." I started becoming acquaintances with some of the more popular girls at school that never gave me the time of day before. It seemed that if I played the part I was given by society, I could fit in.

Things changed when I left for college and was allowed room to breathe. For the first time in my life, I felt I could explore every aspect of myself and find what was truly "me," as opposed to what had been forced onto me by others. This was also when I became a sex worker. Not only did I become a sex worker, but I also discovered things like black metal, things that I had shied away from on my quest to appear as feminine as possible. Finally, I had begun to come into my own once more. Every photo set and video I shot, I put on a new performance, and at first, it was easy. When I was just starting out, no one had any expectations of me. My hair was short, I never wore make-up, I didn't try to be someone I wasn't. However, that only lasted a couple of years.

I began to fixate. Fixate on what every other person around me was doing. Fixate on the flowing hair of the other alternative models. Fixate on their pristine make-up, on their huge lips, on their form-fitting clothing. I decided I needed to perform that kind of femininity if I was going to really make it in the adult industry. I grew my hair out, began wearing make-up every time I shot, started wearing fewer t-shirts with jeans and more sexy lingerie. I became hyper-focused on the feminine, the very thing I had been trying to break away from for so long. The difference was that now I was my own worst enemy. This became exponentially worse when I began camming in 2016, four years into my sex work career. The focus on my body during a live stream became overwhelming. Especially the focus on my breasts. The comment after comment about them made me hyper-aware of my body dysphoria. This was what finally allowed me to open my eyes to the reality of the situation. The reason I pushed aside anything feminine, the reason I felt I had to perform womanhood, the reason I was so uncomfortable about people talking about my breasts, it was all because I wasn't cis. It was such a simple revelation and it was such a complicated revelation all at once. It plowed into me like a train. I didn't know what to do with the realization. I sobbed. I panicked. I cried to my boyfriend in the middle of the night and asked if he'd still want me (thankfully, he did). And then I became euphoric.

I came out to the internet almost immediately. I believe it was a mere two days between my breakdown and me confiding in everyone on Tumblr, as was usually the case (RIP). That same day, someone offered to buy me a $60 binder. No gesture of gift giving has ever been appreciated as much as that was, and the second it arrived, I took thousands of pictures in it. I felt like the old me had died and like a phoenix, I had been reborn into a person I could respect and cherish. However, things were not all rainbows and sunshine. I was still a sex worker, and I still had to perform. The hardest thing was returning to cam. MyFreeCams only allows "female" performers and so I began to act. I acted like the most feminine female to ever female. Only a select few of my regulars were allowed in on the truth, and one of them tried to convince me I was wrong and just needed more time to reflect. He was also in love with me and clearly couldn't stand the thought that his already unattainable "dream girl" was never really a "girl" at all. This led to my eventual realization that perhaps camming on a site like MyFreeCams was not the ideal choice for me, and thus, I quit to start a vanilla career on the side.

Leaving MyFreeCams was one of the healthiest choices I have made thus far in my sex work career. Now when I perform in a video or in a set, I can truly focus on my performance. I don't have to focus on people questioning me or my gender and misgendering me every other sentence. I can take mental health breaks to regroup when my dysphoria becomes too much. My heart and soul go into the art of sex work instead of into the back and forth with clientele. Now when people question my identity, I can answer them with the buffer of internet text and no longer feel like I have been placed on the spot in an extremely vulnerable position.

The Espi Kvlt that appears in my sets and videos is a woman that uses she/her pronouns. She is a woman confident in her sexuality and her body. She is a woman that loves to get off and is horny all the time. She knows what men want and she's prepared to give it to them. The Espi Kvlt of reality is a nonbinary person that uses they/them pronouns. They are a person confident in the realities of their dysphoria and confident in their gender identity. They are a graysexual person who loves to make porn and turn that love into art they can be proud of and share with the world.

From the age of 14, I already knew I wanted to do porn. What I did not realize, however, was how much of an effect my gender identity would have on it. It would have been so easy to continue bottling it away for the sake of my career and the perception others have of me. It would have been so easy to simply give up on sex work the moment I realized the truth about myself.

However, I am a fighter, and although I needed to make compromises for my mental health, I am now more comfortable and happier in my own skin than ever before. I am nonbinary. I am a sex worker. I am Espi.

Unconventionally Attractive

By Blake Noble (he/him)
Content warnings: *sexual activity*

I'm fat
and the weight of me pushing you into the mattress,
against the wall,
over the edge
leaves you breathless.

I'm fat
and my chest meets yours
long before our lips can touch.
You feel your body become flush with mine,
my breath grazes your neck
and you can't help but pucker
as you anticipate the softness of my chin
brushing your skin
when my greedy tongue
finally finds your insides.

I'm fat
and I'm so hot
even the shadow I cast
over you is warm.

I'm fat
and I have a gravity
which pulls you ever closer to me.
You long to cross that event horizon
into a dimensionless space
where our flesh is infinite
and without borders.

I'm fat
and the dimples in my ass and thighs
make me look like a Pointillist masterpiece.

I'm trans.
You see the way I fuck with gender
and you think to yourself
"I want some of that".
Well, I hope you like it rough.

I'm trans
and it's not just the intrigue in my pants.
It's the magic in my fingers,
the lust in my lips,
the teasing in the tip of my tongue
and the electricity in my teeth.

I'm trans
and my appeal cannot be contained
in any number of ones and zeros.
My queerness is off the charts.
And the Venn diagrams I make with you
will never fit on one page.
I will not be tethered
to any one base or alphabet.

I'm trans
and my biology is the stuff of fantasy.

I'm trans
and my body is gloriously unburdened
by arbitrary boundaries.
A tide gushes out of me with enough force
to wash away anything which doesn't belong.

I'm trans
and I'm too sexy for my society.

I'm disabled
and no one gets to fuck me "in spite of" my impairments
even though sometimes
I decline to be fucked because of them.

I'm disabled
and my pride in my inability to function
as capitalist society expects me to
makes you blush.
Let's reinvent beautiful together.
Let's make it so that tonight
the wetness on my cheeks
is because of the thrill I inspire in you
not the anguish they inspire in me.

I'm disabled
and I pledge to let love in.
I will endeavour to love myself
when I masturbate.
There will be no guilty pleasures for me,
only self-care and a willingness
to see myself as deserving.

I'm fat, trans and disabled
and you love it.

Dating While Genderqueer

By MJ Jonen (they/them)
Content warnings: *sexual assault, sexual activity*

Navigating sex, sexuality, and relationships as a non-binary person has not been easy. Most people don't understand what being genderqueer, or non-binary in general, is all about. I didn't even know that non-binary genders existed until my first semester of college. The development of my sexuality, my relationship with gender dysphoria, sexual trauma, sex, and the realization that I am polyamorous have all been huge factors in my everyday life. I wouldn't be who I am today without all of the stumbles, all of the education, and all of the experiences that I have under my belt (no pun intended).

First, an introduction. My name is MJ and I am a non-binary genderqueer and otherwise queer individual. I wasn't born MJ, though. I was born under a different name, assigned female at birth, and raised as a girl. Like I said earlier, I didn't even know that being non-binary was a possibility until I was halfway through my eighteenth year, so when I heard about the term transgender in early high school, I didn't think that was me. I knew that I wasn't a guy, so I must have been a girl, right? Wrong. I was very wrong. For a long time, I struggled with gender dysphoria, though I didn't know that that's what it was at the time.

My sexuality is and has always been, as fluid as my gender. I've been out as some sort of queer since middle school. I didn't use that term back then, though. In fact, I still considered it a slur and hated when other people used it. Needless to say, I have grown since then. I first came out as bisexual. Thinking back, I have an inkling that the only reason I came out as bi and not gay was that society had trained me to like guys. From then, up until my first semester of college, I was out as bi, but it wasn't ever talked about and people, even my friends, tended to 'forget'. Then college came along and almost all of my new friends were some sort of queer. That, along with the fact that I went to a women's college, led to me coming out as a lesbian. At that time, before I had learned of non-binary genders, that's the identity I felt confident in.

I didn't immediately start questioning my sexuality when I began to settle into my non-binary identity, and I think that really helped. It wasn't until about six to seven months after I came out to everybody that I started at a new school and developed a sexual crush on a guy. This really didn't faze me at all. I had a view of sexuality that was very flexible, and I had accepted the fact that I might not only like women for the rest of my life. That crush didn't work out, but I still kept my options open. Since then, the only people I have dated or had sex with have been people with vaginas. I'm just more comfortable that way. At my second college, I got into some friends-with-benefits relationships but due to dysphoria as well as sexual trauma, I would only ever be the one giving never on the receiving end. I thought that this was what I wanted but, in all truth, it's not who I am.

It would take another year and a half before I would let somebody do anything to me. I would still get a lot of dysphoria and the effects of my trauma would be triggered sometimes, but I pushed through. Then, I was sexually assaulted again and was thrown back from how far I had come. I closed myself off, which didn't help the relationship I was in. Healing from sexual assault only complicated the relationship I had with my body, with sex, and by extension, with my girlfriend. Not only was my girlfriend questioning her identity as a lesbian due to dating me, a non-binary individual, but now she was in a relationship that had started out very sexual and now wasn't sexual at all. I began, once again to identify on the asexual spectrum. I had done this before, and it never fully went away due to my first assault and my dysphoria. Asexuality brought on by trauma or by dysphoria is just as valid as asexuality that is innate in a person. It took me a long time to come to terms with this, so I feel it is important to state whenever this topic arises. I still identify on the asexual spectrum to this day.

Since then, I have done a lot of recovery work with a therapist and with more recent partners. Part of this has been affected by my introduction to and exploration of kink. I have found that plain, vanilla sex is too boring for me. I get stuck in my head and that's when I get dysphoric and that's when my trauma is triggered. With kink, my body is being so stimulated that my brain overflows with endorphins and I can enjoy sex. Without spicing things up in bed, I don't think I could ever be as sexual as I am now. Safe, sane, and consensual kink has allowed me to overcome my dysphoria.

Another part of my life affected by my identity as a non-binary person is dating in general. I find it very hard to date because I am polyamorous, also known as 'ethically non-monogamous'. The way I define polyamory for myself is the ability to love openly and freely. This means that I can fall in love with and/or date more than one person at a time. When done the right way, ethically, this is not cheating. My partners, past and present, have all been fully aware that I am polyamorous, and are supportive of it. Many have also already identified or have come to identify as polyamorous. While I have tended to open my dating pool to men to expand my possibilities and chances of finding someone, the fact that I am polyamorous narrows that back down significantly. People tend to avoid dating people that are polyamorous because of jealousy. They, mostly, incorrectly assume that one must not ever feel jealousy in order to be in an open relationship or a polyamorous one but that is not the case. Jealousy is a natural emotion. You just have to know how to deal with it and act accordingly. You have to take a step back and evaluate if the source of the jealousy is founded or not, if it has a healthy root or not.

Being non-binary makes dating hard enough without being polyamorous. People typically assume that I am a man, which makes trying to date queer women tough. I say queer women because most straight women, in my experience, are less open to dating a non-binary person. This may very well not be the case in other people's experiences, but I can only state things from my point of view. I have tried dating apps and a website or two, but it hasn't led to anything. I've had two dates from an app in the however many years of usage and swiping and tapping I've done. Most dating sites work on a binary algorithm. Even ones that have more gender options still sort based on which of the two binary genders you feel most aligned with. So, if I say I'm mostly aligned with "manhood", I can either see mostly straight women or mostly gay men. If I say I'm aligned with "womanhood", I can see mostly gay women or mostly straight men. This becomes even more difficult because I am not androgynous. I look very masculine and, most of the time, I wear masculine clothing. I also have facial hair now. So, how does a person like me, with facial hair, go on these sites with the woman-aligned option selected and hope for success?

Overall, dating and sex as a non-binary person have been a rough road, especially considering my past sexual assaults. I have come to rely on potential dates coming from friends or acquaintances. It's rare that I date someone I haven't already known for a little while. Sex, for me, has gotten better over time. People grow, people learn, people explore new sides of themselves all the time. There's always hope. There's always someone or some people. My advice: talk to people and get to know them. Who knows where that will lead?

Nonbinary Butch

By Amber Auslander (they/them, he/him & she/her)

Hair cut short, slicked back, wearing a pair of thrifted slacks and making your heels click on the sidewalk, loud enough for everyone to see you, so gloriously, so handsomely in between.

Fig. 16 by Jayse Hamend (they/them)

Unshackling The Binary

By Nyx McLean (they/them)
Content warnings: misgendering

People make sense of the world through categorising it. It may be explicit but more often than not it is unconscious. The cisgender world is dominated by a need to split humxns into two gender categories: man, woman. After years of socialisation, it is not surprising that some trans folk appear to be doing the same thing to each other. I have found myself 'gendered' while still having my non-binary identity acknowledged, this occurs because people unintentionally assign a perceived gender identity to our bodies. I have also seen how other non-binary folk are encouraged to present their identities in a certain way.

Gendering Non-binary

Some trans folk tend to add a perceived assigned gender at birth (AGAB) to the identifier 'non-binary' when referring to myself and other non-binary people. I noticed that over the last few years that language started to shift towards AFAB and AMAB identities. Some of my trans peers would introduce me as an AFAB or AMAB non-binary person. I thought nothing of it until someone I knew fairly well began to misgender me regularly – using the incorrect pronoun for me despite having known me for the last five years.

My pronoun had not changed since the time we met while theirs had changed numerous times, and each time I used the correct pronoun for whichever stage they were at or identity they were moving through the world with. What I found strange here was that while mine had stayed fairly stable they were unable to remember which pronoun to use, while although theirs had been in flux, I was able to keep track of their pronouns. I figured that what it came down to was how we perceived the world, and how much we have actively deconstructed the fixed categories of gender.

I do not believe that trans folk who misgender other trans folk do so maliciously, only that their worldviews are still closely aligned to a binary world. Even though they may know that multiple genders exist their socialising has not quite caught up, and so the wrong pronoun slips out because a gender has been assigned to someone on the basis of what they've been told particular bodies look and sound like.

I've taken to addressing this unwanted gendering of my body by trans peers as soon as it happens. I believe it is best to reveal the discomfort and unpack it rather than to mull it over and let it form a layer of resentment. We can both learn in that moment if we are willing to ask and to listen. There is courage in calling attention to harmful practice, and there is courage in being willing to listen, respond honestly, and reflect on why poor gendering behaviours persist.

Non-binary Prescriptive Presentations

In spaces, both online and offline, I noted that a pattern emerged in the initial burst of non-binary identities: communities began to cultivate a particular non-binary aesthetic. While rejecting binary gender identities the communities were encouraging a particular 'gender' performance for non-binary and gender non-conforming folk. One that appeared to be associated with masculinity.

By this, I mean that masculine presentations were favoured and encouraged. People who presented themselves in an androgynous and often masculine way were greatly affirmed in comparison to those who leaned towards feminine presentations. Such spaces come to be exclusionary of more feminine presenting non-binary folk. And with this, I noticed that the number of feminine presenting folk sharing images of themselves online dwindled until not a single share could be found.

One must question what is at play here when dress and makeup are rejected if they lean too close to the gender identity of "womxn" while those leaning more towards masculine presentation are celebrated. Part of the reason for this may be how AFAB nonbinary people are overrepresented in comparison to AMAB nonbinary people coupled with cissexist expectations to "prove" you have no ties to your assigned gender. Furthermore, dysphoria caused by frequent misgendering can lead to a desire to present more androgynously - but the culture's idea of androgyny leans towards the masculine. While it is understandable then to present in a way that demonstrates social ties to a certain group and that minimises dysphoria, we must recognise that this is still occurring within a society that only deems predominantly white, male and able-bodied identities worthy of respect, and is not immune to these influences.

I do not think that this was intentional but rather it is a symptom of a binary world which favours the masculine and the power associated with it. The ideological power of patriarchy is so strong that a community of people who outright reject binary gender identities have inadvertently come to adopt or celebrate identity presentation that leans towards a binary gender identity, and one that holds a particular power position. One must ask then if it is a matter of non-binary folk siding with power. This is not a criticism but rather an understanding that, if it is the case, that this makes sense in this world where it is already dangerous to simply be a person who is not a cisgender heterosexual man. To favour masculine presentation may simply be about accessing power and, with it, a safety that is not otherwise available to those who do not fit neat gender categories.

Non-binary As A Rejection Of Categories

It is easy to fall into gendered ways of speaking and thinking. I had to unpack for myself what it meant to write about masculine or feminine clothing, hair, presentation and whether I was speaking about gender or speaking about a presentation aligned to a particular identity or identity characteristics. And what this means for future ways of speaking about identity. How do we describe a way of being without assigning a binary gender expression to it?

This short essay was trickier to write than one would think. I'm an academic by training and I tried to challenge myself to write outside of that "genre", to move away from texts to cite and to embed myself within academic fields. It was damn near impossible at times. It had me thinking about how similar learning to move in a different way with words was to the first time I openly acknowledged that I was a non-binary person in a very binary world. There are codes for how to think, talk, dress, eat, and be in the binary world. But outside of that, the part that is truly terrifying - and later liberating - there are no codes. The only true code is to get to know yourself and move in a way that makes you comfortable, the way that resonates with your spirit. From there, you decide how you want to move through this world.

For me, to be non-binary is to reject gender. To disrupt, to refuse, and to not stand down. What being non-binary is perhaps asking of us is to reject these easy labels and to get on living in ways that are not restricted by tight unmoving social categories. It is asking for courage to simply exist – no excuses, no explanations. To live queerly and to live with courage.

Strut

By Dyceria Tigris Corvidae Satchwill (she/her)
***Content warnings:** transphobia*

I strut
heeled boots and narrow skirt determine my pace.
I strut
spine straight and shoulders back.
I strut
push-up bra and too-tight camisole restrict my breath.
I strut
painted nails and painted face.

Do you see
my beauty past the beard,
the deepened voice
brought forth by multiple punctures of the thigh?
Do you see
there is no regret here,
no de-transition
only multiple truths layered one atop another?
Do you see
the equal parts fear and disdain
of your opinion of me
as we pass each other on the street?

Every encounter is a risk.
Identification marked "x" lends validity
but little protection
should you decide this white skin
does not make me enough like you
to let me live.

Still I strut

spine straight
shoulders back.
I offer you a smile
and show no fear.
I strut.

How Ordering A Coffee Made Me Question My Gender

By Theo Hendrie (he/him & they/them)
Content warnings: *misgendering*

The day began with the traditional wake-up call: coffee. It was comforting in its overwhelming familiarity; the same off-white walls, minimalist aesthetic and pervasive odour of coffee beans that existed in every Starbucks I'd ever stepped foot in. And then I was given my drink and suddenly it didn't seem quite so inviting anymore.

I couldn't bring myself to laugh, looking at the paper cup with its stark Sharpie scrawl. 'Thea,' it declared. It would have been irrational to march back up to the counter and explain that "Actually, my name is 'Theo' like with an 'O', as in the masculine name," and yet that's exactly what part of me wanted to do.

My friend tried to commiserate with me, showing me the missing "h" off the end of the "Hannah" scrawl on her cup. I appreciated the effort but the missing letter still left her with the right name and the right gender. As far as coffee shop mishaps go, it seemed to me that she had got off lucky.

You see, this didn't feel like a simple spelling mistake. Names are after all, how we communicate to the world who we are so to be told without words that I don't look like a 'Theo,' and that I must instead be a girl with a girl's name is a slap in the face. Such a simple mistake can feel like a denial of who I really am because even though I had no reason to formally come out to the barista, my chosen name is an extension of that identity.

It's not just the coffee though. Many of my day to day interactions - in the supermarket, in the street, in the pub - seem to go this way. Most of the time I am tense and waiting for it, the moment when a "lady" or "girl" or "she" or "her" or "miss" or "ma'am" will slip through the cracks and remind me how the world sees me. In this hugely binary world, the reality is that most people are going to see me as a young woman as they sort each stranger that they see into the "man" or "woman" category without conscious thought.

I tell myself often that it had been worse before I changed my name but in many ways the impact is different. Before, at least I could console myself that the name itself was feminine and they could hardly be blamed for jumping to conclusions. Now, I am finding that people assume my gender incorrectly, in spite of my name and not because of it.

"Why don't you spell it out for them when they ask for your name?" my friend suggested.

"I don't want to have to do that," I told her "I shouldn't have to tell them."

"Well... what do you want?"

I didn't have to think about the answer to that for long: I wanted people to stop seeing me as a woman when they looked at me. That triggered my gender dysphoria, the feeling of intense discomfort that can be caused by the disconnect between a trans person's true gender and how the world sees them. As I thought about it though, I realised that the few times I had been perceived as a man hadn't given me that same stricken feeling.

When a little boy had pointed at me and shouted: "he's got blue hair." The time standing in line, when an older man had squeezed past saying: "Excuse me, sir." Even standing in the club with my friend, under the flashing red and purple lights, the night that she had chipped her tooth, as she had been asked: "Is he bothering you?" And I had felt... glad. Not just that there

182

was someone there to look out for my friend but that someone had seen me that way.

My mind reeling with all these new realisations, I began to question whether being seen as a man could give me gender euphoria.

Up until that moment, I had only used singular 'they' pronouns and asked that people used gender-neutral language when referring to me. Even, the name "Theo" despite being more commonly associated with the masculine "Theodore" had been chosen because it could also be short for the feminine "Theodora." I liked the duality of that, the possibilities that it opened up.

When I first began questioning my gender and asked that friends and family used 'they/them' pronouns for me, it had been so instrumental in lessening the dysphoria that I had struggled with for years that I never stopped to think if any other pronouns might also work for me. I had found something that worked after being so unhappy for so long, and I had stuck with it. Sitting there with my coffee, however, I began to wonder if maybe I had been wrong. Maybe being completely gender-neutral wasn't the only way forward for me.

Back home, I tentatively raised the idea with my boyfriend that I might like to start using 'he/him' pronouns alongside 'they/them.' He had already handled not one but two comings out during our relationship, first as bisexual and later as nonbinary, but it felt harder to tell him that I might have been wrong about which label suited me best.

I needn't have worried: he agreed right away. And from then on I began to hear a mixture of neutral and masculine language. He still called me his partner, but he called me a guy too. I had thought it would feel strange but it didn't.

183

From there, it was simply a matter of untangling the complicated web that is gender. I had been proudly open as an androgynous nonbinary person and the label nonbinary still felt right to me. But I was beginning to realise that my gender-neutrality had more to do with what I wasn't than what I actually was. I knew that I didn't fit completely into the gender binary. And I knew that I definitely wasn't a woman, regardless of what I had in my pants. So, I had settled for the first label I came across that captured that much but what was I leaving out?

I grabbed my laptop and began to trawl the internet, in search of the answers to all the questions that ordering coffee had dragged up. It was then that I stumbled across the label transmasculine. It described so many things: someone who aligned themselves with men or who was partially but not wholly a man or even someone who was both a man and nonbinary all at once. Someone who wished to be part of a community with trans men in order to discuss shared issues. Someone whose transition would follow an "FTM" path. Someone like me.

Claiming, the label transmasculine let me be all of myself with nothing left behind. Gender-neutrality had been a temporary fix, a plaster taped over a wound much too big for it. This me feel whole in a way I hadn't for years. I didn't have to pick a binary gender. But I didn't have to ignore the parts of me that were aligned with the binary either. And best of all, it gave me access to a community and resources that could help me figure out what medical options for transitioning might be right for me. I was home.

The next time I went in for coffee, I was paranoid about my voice, my body, my face. I had worn trainers, jeans, a men's t-shirt and an oversized flannel, hiding the softer curves of my body. Underneath, I had a binder, constricting my chest into something flatter, more masculine. I had done all I could.

Standing in the line, behind a couple picking out sandwiches, I coughed and cleared my throat multiple times, trying to speak from my chest. When I ordered, I winced at the way my greeting automatically drifted into a cheerful upswing that couldn't have sounded less manly if it tried. And I comically overemphasised the O, making my name not "Theo" but "TheOoo".

It didn't work. The barista still called out "Thea" and I burned with shame as I went to collect my drink. The "a" in thick, black sharpie scrawl stared back at me, stubbornly.

The problem was, changing my labels wasn't going to be enough to change how everyone around me saw me. I had already known that I needed to do more than change my clothes, hair and name if I was ever going to be gendered correctly without first beginning the laborious process of coming out and answering questions and patiently correcting mistakes. This only confirmed it and led to one more realisation: I think I'm ready to begin my medical transition.

The simple act of ordering coffee led me to so many questions about myself. Why did I choose a boy's name and wear a man's clothes and want to pass for a guy if I'm so nonbinary? One answer only led to more questions and definitions but I can say it proudly now: I'm a nonbinary man. I am a guy but I don't fit fully into the binary because gender is complicated as fuck and I get to make the rules about who I am.

Maybe one day, I'll be able to pass as a man. At least then, half of who I am won't be erased. At least then, they might write "Theo" on my coffee cup.

185

Changing Academia

By Shelby K. (she/her & they/them)
Content warnings: *transphobia*

As I write this, I am heading to a PhD interview, for which I plan to wear a pantsuit and Oxfords with painted nails and big earrings. I have found this is a way to, more or less, present as my fully nonbinary self in a professional, academic context. But as a current master's student, I have found that entering graduate school as a gender-nonconforming person is an entirely different experience from exploring gender identity in college. I think that the reason for that lies primarily in the fact that once you become a graduate student, you are truly a professional academic. You teach and generate research. You are fully an adult, and at least for the time being, school *is* your career. This is the point where, if you're lucky enough, you can actually be compensated for your academic labor. Along with taking your place in the halls of the academy come a number of expectations placed upon who or what you can be - are *allowed* to be - as an academic.

One unfortunate reality about academia is that it is resistant to change. Trying to change structural pieces of academia is always a challenge, as I've learned from my history as a student organizer. I still remember being an undergraduate asking the president of the university to divest from fossil fuels and being dismissed along with the hundreds of students who made the same demand before and after me. The cynical, but not inaccurate, view is that in academia in general, people in positions of authority want to feel progressive, like they're doing the right thing, but are unwilling to make structural change. In order to understand why, I think it's necessary to explore both the history of academia and how it currently functions.

The history of the university is one of exclusions, where only the wealthiest members of white society could gain admittance, and where heterosexuality and gender conformity were mandates. As a result, the university in its structure is a rigid and binary space. That is why being non-binary as a burgeoning academic can be quite a challenge. When I entered my master's program, I was still in a state of questioning my identity, but I had become fairly confident that I wasn't a woman, and I had always been pretty certain that I wasn't a man (I'm AFAB and while that doesn't sit quite right with me, I'm pretty sure being assigned male would have been even less preferable). When I arrived, I realized that the space for me to be my gender non-conforming, questioning self was simply not there. The entire department was located high up in a building with one gender-neutral restroom, which was in the basement. I learned that there had previously been some resistance to the idea of installing a gender-neutral restroom closer to the department itself. So, I had two choices: run down three flights of stairs whenever I needed to use the restroom or use the women's room. I chose the latter out of necessity. There just was never time to make it downstairs and back between teaching, going to class, research meetings, office hours, and so on. I remember hearing, around that time, the idea that if there is no bathroom for someone to use, the message is that they are not welcome in that space. I was getting the message that the only version of me that was accepted in my department was a closeted version, pretending to be a woman. I tried not to internalize it too deeply, but to this day when I use that restroom, I get a sense of embarrassment, because I feel as though I am misgendering myself in front of all my female colleagues.

I started to do more in the way of transitioning after I started my master's, and I think part of that was me subconsciously pushing back against the social dysphoria I had not experienced until that point. I began using 'they/them' pronouns exclusively in my professional email signature, displayed pronoun stickers on my desk and laptop, started binding some days and wearing more men's clothing, and buzzed all my hair off. These are things I had never really felt the need to do until becoming a grad student - until I entered this rigid environment with all these gendered and binary expectations placed on who or what I should be as an academic.

When you're made to feel "other" in some way, or when you're made to feel like your identity doesn't belong in a specific institution or area, it's unfortunately easy to get into the mindset that asking for basic respect is too much of a burden on others. At times I have felt like asking professors or fellow graduate students to remember my pronouns was asking too much, that they had too much else to worry about to think about using the right pronouns for me. But for cis people using the correct titles or honorifics or pronouns was a matter of course. I still have only actively corrected someone on my pronouns once, but I'm working on being just a little more visible as a non-binary grad student, in an attempt to make space for any nonbinary people that may enter my department in the future.

So, in terms of how the institution we know as the University works today, the way that they sustain themselves, of course, relies on money. That money comes from a lot of sources, but one major stream of income for universities, at least in the US, is their students and their students' families, between tuition and donations from alumnae. This means that universities need to make wealthy families want to send their children and donate to their institutions. Courting wealth, especially what is seen in the US as "East coast elite" wealth, oftentimes means appearing "respectable" and "apolitical." While some view academia as a "far-left cesspool," or something along those lines, the reality is that if academia is liberal, it is neoliberal, with all the connotations of capitalism and centrism that implies. I have seen university administrations ignore and minimize expressions of white supremacy on campus out of a desire to maintain an outward appearance of "moderacy" and "listening to both sides."

So how does this concern for appearances and respectability concern non-binary identities? Well, one issue related to gender expression is the idea of professionalism. I have lots of problems with the concept of professionalism itself. Generally, it is exclusionary to people who have access to fewer resources, and there are people who, by nature of bias surrounding their identity, are automatically viewed as less professional and have to try even harder than their peers to be taken seriously (I see you, academics of color). Professionalism is also strictly gendered, especially in terms of appearance. If you are perceived as female, you wear makeup and high heels to an interview. If you are perceived as male, you wear a tie. Flip any of that and it is automatically seen as less professional. I plan to challenge the norm just a bit with my aforementioned interview attire (in particular, wearing Oxfords instead of pumps), although I know I will usually be read as female regardless.

With being non-binary, there is also the issue of having an identity that is politicized. I am politically active, as are many members of the LGBTQIA2S+ community. This is most likely because we, along with other marginalized groups, are more impacted by political changes and perhaps more likely to object to systems in general. However, even in situations where we don't want to be, people with queer identities, especially trans and non-binary identities are considered political inherently. Right now, at this political moment, where major political battles are being fought over our identities, to have the same rights as cis citizens and even our right to use the bathroom, our existence is considered political. That means our existence is antithetical to the apolitical academic institution. In addition, when we are generating research and other works of scholarship, those of us with politicized identities often experience being perceived as less objective. For example, my field is psychology, and on the subject of gender dysphoria, I am seen as biased in thinking it shouldn't be considered a disorder because I'm a member of the group impacted by it. But my personal experience with the issue doesn't necessarily make me less objective than a cis person with their own perspectives and experiences, or lack thereof, with gender nonconformity especially when many have transphobic biases. It simply lends a first-hand perspective that isn't often given to this particular issue.

I don't want it to seem like I am condemning universities as always being a negative experience for queer people when often the opposite is true. When I first went to college at eighteen, I wasn't "out" in any way, but the way that I was welcomed by straight and queer members of the community at my college made me feel free to first come out as bi, and later on, start exploring my gender identity. At my undergrad, I didn't feel pressured to be visible in any particular way or to make it easier for other people to understand me. I had more of a sense that I could still be nonbinary even if I had long hair and wore maxi skirts or went by 'she/her' pronouns sometimes. And even though it has been harder during my master's program, transitioning has not been a problem for me on an individual level. I've had professors thoughtfully ask about my pronouns and preferred title (Mx., though the gender-neutral title I aspire to is Dr.) to make sure that they were using the correct language in my recommendations. There are many people involved in academia who don't just want to appear progressive but actually, make progress. And as more openly queer, trans and gender-nonconforming people enter the academy and make waves, and more of those people who want to make change organize together, I believe that academia can be radically rebuilt.

The Strength Of Broken Glass

By Lee Seater (they/them)

I am not strong.
I am glass-brittle
- sharp shards to slice you to the bone.
But I am not strong.
I am not your good example.
I am not your inspirational quote.
I don't ask anybody
to look up to me
- I don't even ask them to look at all.
I'm tired and bitter and
I am not strong.
My voice dies in my throat
- I don't shout out to lead us all.
I cry a lot.
I look at myself and wonder
if there's a self yet to discover
a me who can stand tall.
I'm small and sour and
I am not strong.
But I've made it this far.
The glass-shards catch the sun sometimes
and look like something beautiful.
I'm trying so hard
- I always have been.
I am not strong
- but I can be strong enough for this.
That's all.

Where Is The Land?

By Andrea (they/them)
*Content warnings: colonialism, racism, genocide, rape
mention*

Non-binary and trans settlers haven't done shit for me.
In the US they have a lot of demands. Where's the
correct gender marker on my birth certificate, where's
discrimination protection, where's the universal
healthcare, proper healthcare, informed healthcare.
Where's my safety, where's my recognition, where's my
employment, where's the understanding, the empathy,
where is it? All good questions, necessary questions.
But as a wíŋkte, I only have one question. Where's the
land?

I've never known my own land. In the 60s, my family
was sent into the diaspora by the economics of being
Indian. A small family in the sea of dispossession and
genocide that the United States created. Grandmama
lived on the rez, moved to Bismark. Had a family,
couldn't find work in Bismark, moved onto Coast Salish
land. The most I've known of my country was a family
vacation we took when I was young. Went to ☐é Sápa,
drove across the Plains, went to Bismark, to the country.
Most settlers who live in the US don't know what it's like
to be part of a diaspora. A diaspora caused by their very
presence, their theft of our land. They took our land,
killed and stole our other-than-human kin, put us in
concentration camps. They burned down our homes,
built new ones, forced us into them, then forced us out.
And so now we're here. Now I'm here. In Washington.
 Washington, one of the great liberal states of the
Sacred Union of 50. Also, one of the most dangerous

193

states to be Native in. 3 of the top 10 most dangerous cities for Native women in the US are in Washington. Seattle, Tacoma, Spokane. Cities that scream out with the pain of 100+ years of occupation, of individual murders and collective genocide. People absolutely hate us here. Us meaning Natives in this case. More specifically Native women. And Native people of non-western genders. People in North Dakota hate us, too. People in Arizona, Oklahoma, New York, Georgia, they all hate us. There's no place to be Native in the US, even though every place in the US is Native land. You can't even be Native outside the US. I've met people from Washington outside the country, in Ecuador, told them I was Native, and the jokes would come rolling in. War whoops, savage jokes, poor jokes, casino jokes. From cis people, trans people, all the same. Anywhere, any time.

But since I'm here, in this hatefully accepting liberal state, I may as well start HRT. It's been something I've wanted to do, and it's easier to start here than other places. Easier, not easy. Months of therapy, conversations with doctors, phone calls and appointment making. Lots of money that I don't have. It's either that or informed consent. So, I go to the therapist. And when I see that therapist, who's maybe trans, maybe cis, maybe non-binary, I have to explain that I'm none of those things, that I exist outside of any western conception of gender. I'm wíŋkte. You do know what that means, right?

You see, in our language, there is no word for sex, gender, or sexuality. We don't make this separation between sexuality and gender that the west does. You understand? No, we're not non-binary, our society has at least 5 gender/sexual roles as it is. But I'm just looking to start HRT, it's not necessary to explain our

194

whole social structure to you, is it? Like you get it? Yeah but no, but we're not trans, we're wíŋkte. We have whole social roles that're hundreds of years old. We give names, make clothes, participate in sundance. You know? Like okay, I'm not trans, I feel fine in my body, but I'd still like the hormones, just cause. Don't make me explain more, I'd just like the hormones, please. Yeah, but you're the one on our land, why do I have to explain our society to you if you're on our land? Just gimmie the fucking form, it's not hard. Is it? Is it that hard to accept that we're not trans? Just fill out the form, you don't need my life story, my people's story, you wouldn't understand.

You don't understand.

And in the therapist, in those deep blue eyes, I just see a body living off of our land. A parasitic people that moved in, removed the people already there. Gorging on our land, our resources, taking them and refusing to give them back. Exploiting those resources for decades, becoming more and more wealthy. Going overseas, killing people in the name of having more and more. Raiding our tipis and arresting us, in 1876, in 2016, at Wounded Knee, at Standing Rock. Killing us and raping us for hundreds of years. And having the audacity to stand on our land, on my land, and not understand my people, my gender? Telling me that actually, I'm trans. Actually, I'm non-binary. Erasing me, stuffing me into this western category of gender. Stuffing me into a binary, or into a non-binary system stuck defining itself through a binary. Doing the work of the state in eliminating our epistemologies, cosmovisions, lifeways, forcing us to think white while being brown. Participating in genocide.

And I storm out of the office.

I remember one morning I opened the Seattle Times to have a look through the newspaper, see what was happening locally. The first story I see. "Nearly every Native American woman in Seattle survey said she was raped or coerced into sex."

Do I care very much about my access to HRT anymore? No, I don't. There's only one thing standing in the way of our liberation as wíŋkte; the United States. I don't want HRT anymore; I want the United States to be destroyed. I want our nations to control our land. I want to not live in fear of me or my family being hurt, being hurt again, for being Native. I want to destroy the possibility of the US having the power to control Indigenous lives the world over. I want the US gone, and I want every settler who hates us, who harms us, who kills or rapes us, I want them all gone. That is my freedom. I don't find my freedom in a doctor's office or on an election form. I find it on the land.

      We're not alike. We both know what it's like to be threatened for wearing a dress, but only one of us knows what it's like to live under occupation. That occupatory government will never come to accept wíŋkte, it can't. All of us dying, us as wíŋkte and us as Native people, is the goal of the United States. It needs our land to spread its imperial-capitalist power all over the world. And so, it's attempted to wipe us out. And admittedly, it's done a good job. If you had already heard the word wíŋkte beforehand, which is a big ask, you probably thought we were just Brown trans people, or Brown non-binary people. And that's settler-colonialism working as intended. The people do the work of the state, the cavalry isn't needed anymore.

      For us to live, to survive, to stop the genocide the US is committing against us, we need the land. We need to destroy the state that wants us dead. We need Indigenous lead work, education, life, so that we can save ourselves from genocide and promote our lifeways among a social structure that wants us dead and gone. We need people who believe in true emancipation, people who believe in putting a stop to genocide, to help us achieve this. The land is our life and future.

So maybe now you better understand why I ask the question... Where's the land?

A Self In Danger

By Eddy Funkhouser (they/them)
Content warnings: *transphobia*

"I am tired of being afraid
to speak my name"
Amir Rabiyah

yesterday my Lyft driver was

confused, suspicious, distrustful
angry

when I was the one to get in his car.
my femme, my body, my tits and hips
didn't fit with his perception of my masc name.
he couldn't comprehend it,
somehow it didn't parse,
even though my picture popped up
on his screen right next to my name.

name, identity, presentation
self

a self with tits and hips, a masc name,
and an increasing feeling of

wariness, unease, defensiveness
danger.

when you're in a Lyft you can't just
get out.
your destination is input,
your journey in another's hands.

to ask to stop, to be let out
seems inappropriate.
(more or less inappropriate
than berating a stranger for their name
it's hard to say.)

but to ask to stop, to be let out
means explaining
that your name is yours.
that your tits and hips are yours.
that he, his

confusion, suspicion, distrust
anger

are his, are wrong.
that he has made you

guarded, uneasy, defensive

in danger.

Where Am I In This Game?

By Jamie Kaiju Marriage (they/them)
Content warnings: *misgendering, nonbinary erasure*

I grew up playing video games. As a 90's kid you either went gaming or you went sports, and I sure as hell didn't feel comfortable in the latter. But when the age of the roleplaying game began one thing was obvious: I didn't feel right playing any of the characters. From the beginning, everyone is shoved into the binary. From Professor Oak's "Are you a boy or a girl?" in *Pokémon*, to every sword and sorcery RPG getting you to choose male or female. Something was wrong. Everyone thought of me as a boy but I sure as hell didn't feel right picking that identity in a game, and while playing as a girl at least wasn't the same role, it still didn't feel right.

It took me until I was twenty-nine to come out as non-binary, because I'd never even heard the term before, let alone gotten to play a game as someone who identified as such. In the age of the indie game, we are slowly changing that. I've played more games in the space of a year that allow me to be someone I identify with than the three decades of my life before now. Games made by people like me, who want their voices heard. From the big game companies though? Nothing.

Non-Binary folks are the 'incidental queer' choice. Only appearing in games as an afterthought and forgotten just as suddenly. Harebrained Schemes gave us the ability to choose our pronouns in *Battletech*, with no reference to those in the game, and still refused to give us a non-binary choice in the *Shadowrun* games - games about cybernetics and magic where surely folks like me would flourish. *Stardew Valley* still needs to be played with a mod if you want to be non-binary and not spend every hour of gameplay being constantly misgendered. *Pyre* and the *Sunless* games give you pronoun/title choice, but never let you explore it further. *The Sims 4* got rid of strict binary options but still picks your pronouns for you based on your body type.

It's hard to get excited when you're stuck on the side-lines the entire game.

One of the biggest problems may be the lack of understanding of what non-binary actually means. It's not just the pronouns we choose or any particular appearance, it's the ability to be who we are. Why should someone who uses 'he/him' pronouns be stuck with an overtly "masculine" appearance? Why do only some people get to wear makeup in character creation? Why is the singular 'they' pronoun so difficult for game developers to put in their style guides?

In 2018 I finally felt at least a little included in *Magic the Gathering* when they not only gave us a non-binary gendered character in Hallar, but they changed their formatting so that every "his or her" was replaced with 'they/them ' (something which should have been done from the start). Of course, Hallar promptly vanished into obscurity because the company didn't give them any real story or prominence, and people still loudly decry the templating change, but every little bit helps, right?

And there's the problem in a nutshell. The belief that scraps of representation are enough to make us feel like part of the story. That a singular 'non-gender-specific' character should make us feel included. That once in a while we get to pick 'they/them' pronouns in a game and that will keep us happy and quiet in the corner.

Non-binary isn't that simple. There is no one way to be non-binary. No one look. No one set of pronouns or title that works. To think otherwise is insulting. We deserve more. And we need to demand more.

Don't give us a binary gender character. Let us build our characters from scratch.
Let us choose our own pronouns. Give us every appearance option to choose from. Folks like me deserve a chance to tell our own tales, not have them told for us. So that kids growing up know that there's more to life than "Are you a boy or a girl?"

So where do we start? Where does the games industry go from here to not only help us feel included but to actually include us? For a start let us tell our own stories. Let a non-binary person write the character of a non-binary person, don't just leave it to cis people and hope they don't mess it up. We've seen how badly companies can ruin a good trans character in how Bioware handled Krem from *Dragon Age* or Hainly from *Mass Effect*. Characters whose only defining characteristics were that they only spoke about themselves being trans.

Representing multiple facets of folks who are non-binary is also vital. Don't just show agender types, let's see gender fluid people, demi-girls and demi-boys, aporagender folks and many more. Demonstrate that being non-binary isn't being one specific model of human pumped out of a factory.

And most importantly, let us be the heroes for once. Let us go on a grand adventure, save the world, steal from the rich, build a crew of other non-binary folks to defeat the dragon. Let us have something that kids confused in their own identity can point at and go "that's me" instead of making us wait years or decades to realise that we aren't the monsters in the shadows after all.

It's hard enough to be non-binary in a world that ignores you at best and actively fights against your existence at worst without constantly being erased. This is the time when we need to be seen not only as part of society but as people doing good in it and making it a better place with our art and stories and experiences. Without the validation that comes from one of the world's biggest media sources, it's difficult to believe we even exist.

We need to change that. We need to demand representation. We need to tell our stories. We need to be heard. We need kids like I was to have hope that there's a place for us. Because without characters to identify with, it can be difficult to know ourselves.

Gender Defined

By Penelope Epple (they/them, e/em & one/ones)

My gender is...

two thousand-years-ago
Julius Caesar anointed himself
with rose scented perfume
but when I do the same,
it is labeled as inherently
feminine.

My gender is...

the printer ran out of
cyan and magenta ink
creating a picture in yellow
that is difficult to see.
I suppose
that is fitting.

My gender is...

not passing enough
for the men's room,
not passing enough
for the women's, either.
This is saddening and scary and strangely
comforting too.
Perhaps,
I was never meant
to pass.

My gender is...

going to trans spaces feels like going to church,
exciting and anxiety inducing
all at once.
What's the difference really?
Either way, someone may tell me
"You are not enough
to belong here."

My gender is.

Isn't that enough?

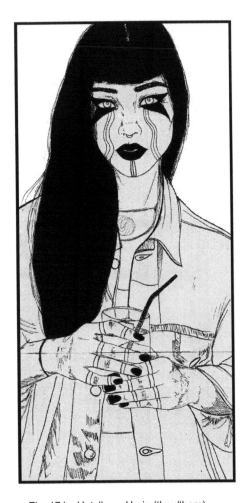

Fig. 17 by Hotvlkuce Harjo (they/them)

Artist Statement:

Hotvlkuce Harjo (they/them), Mvskoke (Creek)
Instagram: @lvstexkvlt

"I'm a non-binary Mvskoke-Creek visual artist based out of Albuquerque, NM. I am currently making working about Southeastern and Mvskoke Tattoo Revitalization. My work re-centers contemporary Indigenous representation through the lens of traditional tattooing. This piece entitled, "MISSISSIPPIAN BLACK METAL GRL ON A FRIDAY NIGHT," reimagines the visual language of the Mississippian era. I utilize the tattoo marking of the lines on the fingers and the face tattoos in this regard. I also take influence from the black metal music scene which also uses facial markings (corpse paint) although in a completely unrelated sense. Black Metal, as well as rock music as a whole, has been a place of refuge for many Native generations due to its ethos going against non-normative systems - making it synonymous with Indigenous lives. This piece also addresses the gender discrepancy in the research around traditional tattooing, especially since those who practiced this are no longer here. When research is conducted under heteropatriarchal systems, gendered labels and roles are attached to these images of my ancestors. Here, I re-constitute the phrase "warrior imagery," a literal truth that the tattoos are battle-related, but more importantly to recognize and pay respect to the feminine/matriarchal structure of Southeastern tribes that was ignored in early research of this region. "MISSISSIPPIAN BLACK METAL GRL ON A FRIDAY NIGHT" is how I imagine our feminine people looking today doing something as simple as going to a show on a Friday night. The spelling of "GRL" was intentional

because it embraces aspects of common everyday language used in conversation for feminine-presenting people but also reclaims (when written out) some of the political identity tied to being non-binary, genderfluid, agender, GNC etc. Because being non-binary is a spectrum this term and it's spelling will work for some folk and others not so much and that's okay. For this piece, I used a technique of pencil line drawings, India ink, and Micron pens."

The Dress

By Dea Ratna (they/them)
Content warnings: *internalised transphobia*

The present-day remake of *One Day At A Time* is, in my opinion, one of the best examples of why remakes and reboots can be a good, and even a great, thing. I enjoy it immensely. But despite that enjoyment, I didn't expect that I, an Indonesian queer human, would have much to relate to in this unapologetically Cuban American comedy.

But oh boy, do I. Other than the coming out storyline of Elena and the presence of one of the very few nonbinary characters on television, I didn't really expect to feel very strongly about a specific scene that, on first glance, has nothing to do with me and my life experiences.

Much of Elena's season one's storyline is about her quinceanera; how she thinks it's a bullshit patriarchal tradition that she wants nothing to do with, contrasted with her mother, Penelope, and especially grandmother, Lydia, seeing it as an important family tradition that they have been looking forward to since Elena was born. And what follows is more or less a typical story of a young teenage girl going through the ritual of becoming a woman by throwing a giant party.

Of course, no quinceanera story would be complete without The Dress.

In all the time that Penelope was planning the quinces, running on no sleep and Cuban coffee, Lydia was busy creating The Dress for Elena. The first time Elena tried it on, she loved it! It was pretty and sparkly, and she felt beautiful. There were smiling faces all around... which upsets Lydia. "This is the wrong dress!"

she declares. Elena was confused. Penelope was confused - Elena liked the dress, the party is tomorrow, so what is her overdramatic abuelita talking about?

Lydia then makes many adjustments to the dress which Elena insists she loves every version of. This scene is very clever upon re-watch. Elena subtly suggests what exactly it is that she wants, maybe so subtly that even she doesn't realize she's doing it.

Hours before the party, Lydia reveals that she has made a few minor adjustments to the dress. Penelope panics about her mother changing something so soon before the quinces - as Elena was in the middle of getting her hair done. Elena takes The Dress from her abuelita and as she unzips it, we see in her reaction the thing that Lydia had been looking for all along. The thing that I felt so strongly about: euphoria.

Elena wasn't smiling and laughing like before. She was crying and laughing. Speechless. all she could do was nod and hug her abuelita. Yes. This was her Dress, which, upon reveal, was not actually a Dress at all, but instead, a beautiful, white, silk Suit.

I remember reading somewhere that being trans shouldn't be about gender dysphoria, it should be about gender euphoria. It shouldn't be about how much you hate being seen as one gender, but it should be about how happy you are being another gender. To me, that moment when Elena looked at the suit, how she was so elated to the point of speechlessness mirrored my own gender discovery.

I never hated being a girl. I never hated wearing skirts and dresses (maybe once during my super tomboy stage), never hated my boobs or my big hips. Never hated that I had a vagina and uterus and ovaries (unless it was menstruation time, then I do hate that they exist). Never hated that I wasn't muscular or bigger

210

or stronger. Never desired to grow a beard. Never feared that my body would change into something I never wanted it to be.

So, if I don't hate it, that means that's what I'm supposed to be, right? A girl?

I was Elena in the first dress that she likes. Yeah, sure, I have no problem looking like this. I look good, actually. Why not look like this for the rest of my life? And then my friends called me handsome when they saw me, and my short boyish hair and I felt euphoria. I felt happy in the way people calling me beautiful never did, though I had never hated being called beautiful.

I started wearing suits and vests with make-up and heels on and people would do a double take. And that made me happy. I would go to a cashier or call a waiter and they'd call me 'sir'. When I started speaking, they'd be confused, and they'd call me 'miss' or 'ma'am'. And I was happy at how much I could fool and confuse them.

And yet, I still struggle to call myself trans. I feel little to no dysphoria, so I feel I don't deserve to call myself that. I just felt happier when people use 'they/them' pronouns for me. I just like looking androgynous most of the time. Wearing binders make me happy, but I would rather not wear it if it's too hot and stuffy. I don't have a dead name and I don't feel dysphoric if someone uses 'she/her' pronouns for me. None of this fit with the trans narrative that I learned about on the internet.

Someone called me a 'trans photographer' recently and I had this strong urge to correct them. It felt like I didn't deserve that adjective. I don't take hormones, I don't need or want gender confirmation surgery, I use the name that my parents gave me, I

211

don't mould my body through painful means to pass as another gender. I don't struggle; hence I don't deserve it. Right? But this one time I let it be. If to them I am trans, then I am. If to them I am not, then I am not.

I'm still not sure if I want to call myself trans or not. At times it feels wrong and at times it feels right. What I do know is that I feel happy straddling the line of the perceived, made up binary. When I do that, I felt like Elena, who never realized that she would feel that euphoria of seeing herself in The Suit, even though she still loved The Dress.

Gender Magic: Finding My Inner Witch

By Jessye DeSilva (they/them)

"When she listened to songs that she loved on the radio, something stirred inside her. A liquid ache spread under her skin, and she walked out of the world like a witch."
- ***Arundhati Roy, The God of Small Things***

One of my earliest childhood memories is of running around in expansive, swooping circles across my back yard. My father was the pastor of a small, conservative, suburban church, and the yard behind the parsonage where we lived was large and lined with trees. Leaping and frolicking through the grass, I perceive myself as lithe and graceful; in hindsight, I was actually a rather clumsy four-year-old with two crooked, protruding front teeth - characteristics for which I had yet to develop shame.

In my memory, I am not playing soldiers or cowboys or even superheroes (that would come soon enough, and even then, I'd be playing superheroines). Rather, I am straddling a crooked, fallen branch, and galloping across the yard cackling, a blanket crocheted by my grandmother for the family couch flopping behind me in the breeze. You see, I've always had a fascination with witches.

As you might imagine, an early interest in the occult - or at the very least, the mysterious women who haunted youthful faerie tales - from a young, male-assigned child of a conservative protestant preacher was not well-received. The predictable concern from my parents was multifaceted. There was, of course, the gender thing. My parents knew long before I did that, I

213

was different, and they were the first to really let me in on the secret of my own "otherness," whether intentionally or not. My interests in art, music, flowers, dresses, flowing hair, and high-heeled shoes were countered with regular encouragement toward sports and masculine role models. And then there was the cultural spectre among mid-1980s evangelical Christians s of "devil worship" and "black magic." This sensationalized view of witchcraft hasn't ever really gone away (see the outcry against *Harry Potter* in the early 2000s).

It was within this social context, where femininity was wrong, magic was heresy, and darkness and otherness were to be feared, that I found comfort and a sense of belonging. Yes, I felt freedom in femininity, but not so much the vapid femininity of the princesses in faerie tales. It was the witches who were my kindred. To me, they were not evil. They were dark, strong, brilliant, beautiful and most of all, misunderstood. In my mind, they didn't just emerge from the womb gleefully plotting the demise of all that is just. No, something happened along the way which led them to question absolute good and to mistrust those for whom everything seemed to go right. Witches embraced another sort of femininity. One that was dark and perhaps even a little bit dangerous. One that had a sharp edge to it. Their femininity was both vulnerable and strong. One might even say it defied the limits of the term itself.

When I was a child, I flew my witch flag loudly and proudly, that is, until I learned that it was a thing to be mocked, a thing of which I should be ashamed. But even then, my inner witch did not disappear completely. She only withdrew to the cover of darkness, like so many other parts of myself.

Soon, music gave me an outlet through which I could embrace the otherness that at times made me feel so isolated. It was through music, during my adolescence, that I once again found my witch. She was there when I ruminated on the absurdity of love with Joni. With her, Tori and I plumbed the depths of darkness, sexuality and pain, and with her, I felt free to embrace the mystical cyclical nature of heartache and joy as I twirled along with Stevie. Only now through music, my witch wove a spell that made me more palatable to others.

In high school, I had a music teacher who encouraged my interests and abilities and gifted me the safety of the microphone and the stage. Here was an altar on which I could lay myself bare, playing and singing my soul while still ending to applause. In college, I studied opera and classical music. During this time, I sang as a countertenor - a cis male singer (as I identified, at the time) who sings in the alto, soprano, or mezzo-soprano range utilizing the falsetto register.

When I chose to pursue the training of my voice as a countertenor, I may not have fully recognized how much of the allure toward such a voice part had to do with its ability to cast a charm on the listener, allowing me to flirt with and bend the limits of gender. Many folks raised in current culture hear an extremely high voice and are reminded of a strict and binary sense of femininity despite the fact that in the 18th and 19th centuries singers of all genders with soprano and contralto voices portrayed characters who were heroic knights and princes, masculine-of-center women warriors, and impetuous young boys, as well as noblewomen, maids, sexually awakened women, and of course, witches. The truth is, in the opera world I felt more like I was in some sort of absurd drag when I was asked to "butch it up" to play Julius Caesar than in the instances when I portrayed feminine roles. Beyond opera, I was drawn to J.S. Bach and G.F. Handel's usage of countertenor voices to narrate scripture, at times speaking with the genderless voices of angels or even as Mary, the mother of Jesus, herself.

Even still, the one musical figure that has never left me has been rock and roll's high priestess, Stevie Nicks. When I first encountered her music and persona there was something odd about her. She seemed to be from another time or world altogether, and yet she was somehow always relevant. She was able to take her otherness and channel it into something that fascinated the general public. Of course, there were rumors of witchcraft, but she never substantiated them, and most folks seemed to brush them off. But I knew - not necessarily that she was a witch in the literal sense of the word, but that she was an outsider. An outsider who had owned this and found a way in.

I think we are in the midst of a cultural moment where many find themselves to be "othered." I don't know that it's a simple numbers game in terms of majority vs. minority so much as the fact that the few have the most - the most power, the most money, and

Fig. 18 by Jackson Burke (he/him & they/them)

the loudest voice. There is something about witches that seems to awaken the otherness in many of us. They are misunderstood. They are seen as dangerous. Their religion was stolen from them and made criminal, and so they practice under the cover of darkness. They find a secret community among one another or they withdraw unto themselves. They take what society teaches should be feared or shameful and they delight in the magic of it all. They believe in the impossible. They practice their craft with sheer will and intention.

I think that there is a bit of witch in all of us. If not, there is certainly something these dark, strong, brilliant, beautiful, misunderstood people can teach us. And so, if you find yourself a "sole practitioner"- if you haven't yet found your coven - know that we are out there. Questioning the powers that be. Singing songs. Weaving spells. Believing in magic.

Queer To The Bone

By Theo Hendrie (he/him & they/them)
Content warnings: *transphobia*

You ask that I put my pride away today
that I talk a little less, take the pronoun
pin off. It's easier, of course, but easier
for who? This way no one asks questions,
this way we don't have to explain my
gender to everyone we meet. But what
you don't understand is that I cannot pack
my identity neatly into a box, I cannot fold
it away with the old clothes at the bottom
of my closet. (After all, I left the closet behind
for a reason). This is a part of who I am
- like the blood in your veins. I carry this
with me even when I am not carrying the
rainbows. This is inside every fibre of my body
because like it or not, I am queer to the bone.

Fig. 19 by Theo Hendrie (he/him & they/them)

Meet The Contributors

Essayists

Andrea (they/them) is a Lak☐óta wíŋkte writer living in occupied Coast Salish land. You can find more writing on being wíŋkte at hinskehanska.wordpress.com or find them as @andrea_lakota on Twitter.

Artie Carden (they/them) is a queer disabled creator with a degree in Creative and Professional Writing. They create stories and content for marginalised people. The arts have always been a passion for Artie, only varying in medium. You can find more of their work at youtube.com/c/artiecarden oartiecarden.wordpress.com.

Castor Santee (they/them) is an alum of the Stephens College Creative Writing BFA program and primarily express themselves through poetry and hair dye. Their writing can be found in the college's literary magazine as well as scrawled on bar bathroom walls.

Charlie B. (they/them) is 19-year-old student from England, working towards a Bachelor's degree in Professional and Creative Writing. They are dedicated to the inclusion of more LGBTQ+ characters in media and hope to someday publish a novel of their own with a diverse cast. Social media for professional work coming soon.

CJ Venable (they/them) is an academic advisor and PhD student in Cultural Foundations of Education at Kent State University (Kent, OH, USA). They work in the intersections of critical whiteness studies, trans people in higher education, fat studies, and philosophical foundations of education. CJ writes and presents on issues of equity, justice, and higher education; you can find them on Twitter as @chrisjvenable. They should probably be reading right now.

Dea Ratna (they/them) is a practising artist currently residing in Singapore. Having been born in Indonesia, the history and culture of Indonesians greatly influences their works. Dea uses the lens-based media, often alongside the written word, to answer one simple question: what is gender? More of Dea's works can be found at dearatna.wixsite.com/dearatna and medium.com/@dearatna.

Donnie Martino (he/him) is a non-binary educator based out of New Jersey. His writing has appeared in *As Told By Things*, *"Music Men Ruined For Me,"* and *Cyberrriot*. He's also the co-host of *I Hope I Can Make It Through: A Degrassi Viewing Podcast*. He's on Twitter as @dmisunbreakable.

Elliot Walsh (he/him) is a full-time writer from Boston and has been writing professionally for over two years. While his job consists of writing on a wide range of subject matter (from marketing tips to scientific discoveries), his writing passions include LGBTQ+ issues, humor, and health. Check out his professional work at walshelliotportfolio.wordpress.com and his personal work at transgrandpa.wordpress.com.

Espi Kvlt (they/them) is a writer who specializes in speculative fiction. They are also an editor in the investigation industry by day and a sex worker by night.

They obtained their B.A. in English-Writing from the University of Nevada, Reno in 2016. They have previously been published in *Gender Terror, The Fem,* and *'n Darkness, Delight.*

Jamie Kaiju Marriage (they/them) is a non-binary lover of giant monsters and all things queer. They write about games from the LGBTQIA+ games industry, stream for queer and mental health positivity, and loudly advocate for representation of marginalised groups in media. You can find their work on Digital Diversity over at enbykaiju.com

Jaz Twersky (they/them) is a nonbinary writer in New York City. They received their degree in linguistics from UC San Diego. They have been previously published in Argot Magazine, the love letter podcast, inewsource, and the Story Seed Vault. For updates on their work, you can find them on Twitter as @WordNerdKnitter.

Jessye DeSilva (they/them) is a singer-songwriter living in Boston, Massachusetts (USA). Growing up as a nonbinary queer person in a religious household greatly influenced their development as an artist whose work often deals with subjects such as family (chosen and biological) and feelings of religious and societal alienation. You can learn more about Jessye's work at jessyedmusic.com.

J.M. Cottle (he/him) is a writer of speculative and historical fiction, a long-distance runner, and a musician. He lives in New Hampshire, happily surrounded by trees. He blogs about philosophy and gender at jmcottle.com.

Jo Newton (they/them) is a student at Calvin College, studying religion, philosophy, and theatre, hoping to become a professional stage manager. They hope to tell stories about what makes us human and our relationship with God, and help others find ways to tell their own stories. Newton has been prolific on social media under various names. You can find more of their work at thenonbinaryknight.wordpress.com, jonewtondoestheater.com or on Twitter and YouTube as @AzariaSpace.

Kayla Rosen is a writer, poet, zinester, and performer based in Seattle, WA. With writing the Seattle Review of Books describes as ""intellectual, political, no holds barred, but also personal, frank, and self-aware,"" Rosen mobilizes memoir as a site for making sense of and healing from trauma. You can find more of their work at kaylarosenzines.com.

K.C. (they/them) is a nonbinary black queer femme who writes about how they navigate the world with their various identities. They are a writer that isn't out in their personal life but tries to be out through their work to make up for that. More of K.C.'s work can be found at ckeys3.wixsite.com/artisticangryqueer.

Keshav Kant (he/him & she/her) is a 22-year old writer from Toronto, Canada. When he's not taking classes at the University of Toronto for Neuroscience and Creative writing, she's one of the main driving forces behind NerdyPoC, an online publication that seeks to amplify Creatives of Colour and give them a platform to share their views on TV, Film, Video Games and other forms of entertainment.

Lu "Ship" Everman (they/them) is a stay-at-home parent, gender-neutral gentleman, and arguably a human. You can find them on twitter @shiphitsthefan where they primarily yell about various fandoms, disability rights, and queer topics. You can also keep up with them with tinyletter (lueverman). They move quickly when caffeinated.

L. Zhu (they/them) is a bi Chinese-American adoptee and psychology major stationed in the Midwest (but with solid plans to move to Oregon in the summer of 2019). This is their first time writing publicly on their non-binary identity and they are honored to be included in this anthology.

Marius Thienenkamp (he/him & they/them) is a 21-year-old English and philosophy teacher trainee from Germany who has been out as non-binary since July 2017. Their passion for American superhero comics, social progress and argumentation got them into writing, and they occasionally contribute articles and podcasts for ComicsVerse.com. Their Twitter account is @mthienenkamp.

Mel G. Cabral (they/them) is a direct response copywriter and content marketer by day, and a creative writer, editor, illustrator, and graphic designer by night. They are an advocate for LGBTQIA+ rights, mental health awareness and support, fair pay for creatives, and productive self-care. In their downtime, they like to craft, cook, and dream up new projects. Their creative hub is melgcabral.com.

Melissa Welter (ze/zir) is a genderqueer activist, writer, and educator from northern California. Ze is a contributor to *"Arcane Perfection: An Anthology by Queer, Trans, and Intersex Witches"* and *"Nonbinary Memoirs of Gender and Identity."* Ze is passionate about creating spaces of justice, healing, and transformation for non-binary and trans folx.

Mika Holbrook (he/him & ze/zir) is a former Cast Member and current Southern Oregon University student, currently debating whether or not he should sacrifice his health to get free Disney passes again.

Mike Levine (they/them) is the author of three books: *Oh, The Flesh You Will Eat!, All The Feelings: Hella Dramatic Monologues For Thespians Of A Teen Age,* and *At Least You're Not These Monsters!* This essay is dedicated to the memory of Danny Lacy, treasured friend and co-author of *At Least You're Not These Monsters!*

MJ Jonen (they/them) is a published writer, poet, and an aspiring playwright. Currently studying creative writing with a minor in women's studies at Stephens College, their work can be found in Wisconsin's Best Emerging Poets: An Anthology and Harbinger Literary Magazine. They also post updates on publications on their Facebook page.

Morgan Peschek (they/them) is an up-and-coming blogger over at akinkyautistic.wordpress.com, a NSFW blog where they write about kink, autism, queerness and polyamory (whenever they're not busy with their BA English course or their knitting).

Nyx McLean (they/them) is a caffeine-fueled queer academic who writes about how queer folk utilise digital spaces to create counter-publics. When not writing they can be found in their garden surrounded by their cats and a squirrel named Pistachio. Online they can be found on Twitter as @NyxMcLean.

Peter Gillet (he/him) lives by a lake in New Brunswick, Canada, with his wife and their two cats. Peter enjoys spending time with friends, walks through nature, meeting new people, and reading the works of many excellent authors. He was the first author registered as non-binary in his province's library system.

RBrown (they/them) writes and teaches in Alabama where they are grateful to be trans and alive. Recent work can be found in *Apogee, Shabby Dollhouse Review*, and others. Their essay, "*A Collection of Unfinished Statements*," was first published by *VIDA Review*. You can usually find them on Twitter as @notalake.

Sandra Lopez (she/her & they/them) is an enby twenty-something from Chicago with a love for reading, writing, drawing, and gaming. They're a committed cat lover and can be found sleeping or pressing their face against their cats' fur. You can check them out on Twitter as @SandraTheDuck.

Shelby K. (she/her & they/them) is a mental health professional and researcher who received their MS in clinical psychology in 2019. Their scholarly work can be found in the University of Minnesota Morris Digital Well, Academia.Edu, and the journals Scholarly Horizons and Archives of Sexual Behavior.

Theo Hendrie (he/him & they/them) is a blue-haired nonbinary YouTuber, writer, artist and poet. Their work focuses on raising awareness of and advocating for trans people and their channel covers everything from looking at current issues through a queer lens, to LGBTQ media recs to teaching the basics of trans identity to confused allies. You can find them anywhere on the internet as @genderpunksap.

Poets

A.E. Greythorne (they/them & she/her) is an indie fantasy fiction writer whose goal is to bring awareness and inclusivity into the arts. A member of the LGBTQIA community, they hope to tell the stories of those who haven't found their voice. Their progress and upcoming releases can be found on Twitter as @aegreythorne.

Dr. Alexandra "Xan" C.H. Nowakowski (they/them) is an Assistant Professor at the Florida State University College of Medicine. Their work focuses on health equity in aging with chronic disease. Lived experience with agender identity, cystic fibrosis, and partner abuse inform their practice. This led them to found the *Write Where It Hurts* project focused on trauma informed scholarship. They have also published poems in HEAL and co-authored the social fiction novel *Other People's Oysters*.

Amber Auslander (they/them, he/him & she/her) is a genderfluid lesbian pursuing Psychology at the University of Pennsylvania. Born and raised in Philadelphia, they are probably happy. Find more of their projects and writing on trans advocacy, polyamory, and lesbian identity on Twitter as @nympheanpink.

Artie Carden (they/them) is a queer disabled creator with a degree in Creative and Professional Writing. They create stories and content for marginalised people. The arts have always been a passion for Artie, only varying in medium. You can find more of their work at youtube.com/c/artiecarden or artiecarden.wordpress.com.

Avi Burton (he/him & they/them) is a 16-year-old American poet. His work has been published in *The Rising Phoenix Review's 'Disarm' Edition*, and *The Voices Project*. Contact him at pentavalence@gmx.com.

Aviel McDermott (they/them & he/him) is an emerging writer who enjoys writing science fiction, fantasy, and poetry. They help run a science fiction/fantasy writing workshop and are president of *Beyond the Binary*, a club for nonbinary students at UC Berkeley. If you're interested in following their writing, you can find them on twitter as @a_the_orange and at softcyberdragonwrites.wordpress.com.

Blake Noble (he/him) is a transnational adoptee trying to find his place in the world. So far, it's been difficult enough making a home in his own body but, with long-awaited access to care, a new relationship and the first published poem of his adult life, things are looking up for him.

Cassandra Jules Corrigan (any pronouns) is a writer and human rights defender originally from Murfreesboro, Tennessee with a Master's degree in International Peace and Conflict Resolution from Arcadia University. They are a member of the queer, disabled, and pagan communities, identify as a genderqueer panromantic grey-asexual and accept all pronouns. Though most of their writing which you can find on their Facebook "Cassandra Corrigan" center on politics and activism, they one day hope to publish fiction and poetry books as well.

David Caggiano (he/him & it/its) is an artist, writer, and musician born and raised in a small town in Kansas. David, or De to close friends and family, is a transmasculine non binary person. More of David's work, including a full-length novel about an LGBT romance, can be found on the website Wattpad as @ActuallySatan23.

Dyceria Tigris Corvidae Satchwill (she/her) was birthed from trauma and this has often been the subject of her originant's art. Now she is creating poetry as a way of healing on her own terms. She shares her consciousness with six other individuals of various genders, which can make for some unique presentations.

Eddy Funkhouser (they/them) is a queer non-binary urban farmer and garden educator living in San Francisco, CA. Their work can be found in Forum, Dirty Girls Magazine, Awakened Voices, Beyond Bloodlines, Stonewall's Legacy, and Written on the Body.

J.J. Hamilton (any pronouns) is an agender and polysexual/bisexual poet, screenwriter, and television producer. Xe uses any pronouns. Xe is from Connecticut and went to school at the University of Miami, studying journalism and film. You can find xem on Twitter and Instagram as @ohheyheyitsjj.

Katie S. (they/them) is a queer non-binary femme tomboy, who's also into roller derby, knitting, coffee, cats, and trying not to be a walking stereotype. They live in Manchester, UK.

Lee Seater (they/them) is a newbie to this whole 'getting published' shebang. They live in Australia with their very scruffy dog, have a weakness for dark chocolate, and have been writing poetry since primary school, though the quality has improved since then. They can be found at leeseater.tumblr.com.

Leo Middlebrook (he/him & they/them) is a 25-year-old nonbinary, bisexual person who stutters, working in education and creating with several mediums including sculpture and writing. His work draws on feelings around self-image, receiving, transformation, and magic. Also gay love. They can be found as @libravenusdreams on Instagram.

Nic Crosara (they/them) is a British freelance writer and self-published poet who has performed all over the South West including at WOMAD festival and Bristol Harbour Festival. Their poetry pamphlet *Tiny Creature* is available now. Their work focuses on media, identity, memory, mental health and social issues but they also have interests in neuroscience, philosophy and cacti.

Olive Dakota (she/they) is a poet and writer who didn't know what to put here, so they asked their friends, who described them as: "soft, brave, strong, the best friend anyone could ask for, an amazingly kind-hearted person, a rabbit lover, and a music enthusiast". Their work can be found @pockmarkedplanet on Instagram and Tumblr and @pockmarkedplant on Twitter.

Penelope Epple (they/them, e/em & one/ones) is a nonbinary aroace poet from Fort Wayne, Indiana, currently residing in Cincinnati, Ohio. They have published work in SOSArt's *For A Better World 2019* and in *Lions-on-Line*, the literary magazine at Mount St. Joseph University. They post poetry as @poetpenelopee on Instagram.

Rain Scher (they/them) is a genderqueer, pansexual, JeWitch activist who lives in occupied Mechoopda territory (aka Chico, CA). They are passionate about Queer Liberation, Intersectional Feminism, and Decolonization. They promised their high school English teacher that if they ever got published, they would dedicate it to Jennifer Tedford "The English Teacher of Infinite Patience."

Red Fawkes (ze/zer) is a white settler of Irish and French-Canadian descent creating art on the unceded lands of the Musqueam, Squamish, and Tsleil-Waututh First Nations, known as the city of Vancouver. Red's art can be found on Instagram as @red.lenore.fawkes.

Rhian Beam (they/them & he/him) is a nonbinary writer and blogger looking to educate on the experiences of nonbinary and genderqueer folks. They hope that one day their blog will become a community for nonbinary people. They dabble in queer poetry as well as writing opinion and experience articles, and they are working on a young adult novel about a nonbinary adventurer. You can find more of their writing at www.nonbinarybirds.blog and can support their work on Patreon @Nonbinary Birds.

Ronnie Vlasáků (they/them) is a twenty-one-year-old nonbinary linguistics and English student from Prague. They love writing poetry, short stories, fanfiction and songs. When they're not writing they enjoy playing Quidditch, jogging, crafts and spoiling their cat. You can find more of their writing at ronnievwrites.tumblr.com.

Mx. Rowan (they/them) is an asexual, aromantic, agender activist with PTSD. They're ethnically Jewish, religiously pagan, and existentially exhausted.

Rune (they/them) is a recent graduate from Coker College, currently residing in Hartsville. They live with their fiancé, Jacob, and the couples' three cats. Rune is currently an English tutor who provides diversity training in their free time. This is their first published piece. They can be found on Instagram as @sam_jean_baguette.

Stephanie (she/her & they/them) is an activist, musician, and writer currently living in Boulder, CO. Their most recent project is cooperating the Rad-ish Collective, a trans-majority housing cooperative and community space. She is a member of Wormfood DIY Music Collective (Denver, CO), and books DIY shows in Boulder, Denver, and Ft. Collins.

T.C. Kody (they/them) lives in Orlando. Their work has been published in *Dream Pop, Voicemail Poems, NAILED Magazine, Button Poetry*, and many others. They are a Best of the Net Nominee. TC's echapbook *Short Poems in the Voice of Birds* is available from

L'Ephemere Press, and they have another forthcoming from Ghost City Press this summer.

Theo Hendrie (he/him & they/them) is a blue-haired nonbinary YouTuber, writer, artist and poet. Their work focuses on raising awareness of and advocating for trans people and their channel covers everything from looking at current issues through a queer lens, to LGBTQ media recs to teaching the basics of trans identity to confused allies. You can find them anywhere on the internet as @genderpunksap.

Artists

A. Alderman (ae/aer & they/them) is a trans and asexual queer artist in the south. Ae likes dogs, aliens, and snails, and right now can be found on Tumblr as @alliterativealmonds and on Deviantart as @activatedalmonds.

Ab Brooks (they/them) is an agender psychotherapy student with way too much time on their hands. They can generally be found skulking around in abandoned buildings or watching pretentious TV shows. If you want to check out any of their other art, you can find them on Instagram as @regretgoblin.

Aiden GD Moore (he/him) is a non-binary illustrator and comic artist currently living with his pet cockroach and hamster, Goki and Butternut Squish, in London, England. He studied Illustration at the University of Hertfordshire and Oita University, Japan. He is best known for his best-selling book *Nihilist Bunnies* and award-winning series *Secret London*. Most often created digitally, his artwork blends themes of sexuality and identity with philosophy and the occult. Other works can be found at aidengdmoore.com.

Andy Passchier (they/them) is a non-binary illustrator from The Netherlands, currently living in the US. By day they freelance children's books and surface design and make short comics about gender and sexuality on the side. More of their work can be found at www.annepasschier.com and on Instagram @annepasschierillustration and @andyrogyny.

Caleris (they/them) likes making all the things, especially colorful things. They're chronically unable to stick to one style or medium, though playful illustrations and geometrical designs are mainstays. Having given up on looking for their path in life, they're now creating their own instead. You can find their work creativeefforts.tumblr.com.

Eireni (Ee-ree-nee) Moutoussi (they/them) is a Greek-English, UK-based digital artist, specialising in environments for game art. Their work can be found at www.eireni.artstation.com, more casually @eireniart on Tumblr and Instagram, and they have a project ongoing at eireni.itch.io/fiscafe.

Hotvlkuce Harjo (they/them) is a non-binary Mvskoke-Creek visual artist based out of Albuquerque, NM. They are currently creating work about Southeastern and Mvskoke Tattoo Revitalization which re-centers contemporary Indigenous representation through the lens of traditional tattooing. You can find more of their work on Instagram as @lvstexkvlt.

IridescentScales (they/them) is the nickname of a self-taught Australian artist who specialises mainly in digital art and watercolour illustrations. The main focus of their art is character drawing and design and their long-term goal is to create and develop webcomics about their original characters. You can find them on Deviantart and Tumblr as @iridescentscales and on Instagram as @iridescentscalesart.

Jackson Burke (he/him & they/them) is a young queer artist who will be attending the Tyler school in Fall 2019. As a transgender person, they understand how important it is to see people like you in art and media and want every trans and nonbinary person to see themselves in art, and to see themselves as a masterpiece, so they use their skills to create art pieces displaying queer bodies and experiences.

Jayse Hamend (they/them) is an artist, musician, and all-round lover of life who's passionate about most anything they can lay their hands on. You can find them on Instagram as @Dromefs and on Twitter as @Dromefz. They want to thank you so much for all your support, whoever you are 🖤

Maddy Test (they/them) is an Aussie animation student with enough enthusiasm to power a city. When they're not drawing collections of fan art and navigating through mountains of WIPs, they can be found wandering the local comic shop or dancing in the rain. You can find more of their work as @witchtonic on Instagram.

Mel G. Cabral (they/them) is a direct response copywriter and content marketer by day, and a creative writer, editor, illustrator, and graphic designer by night.

They are an advocate for LGBTQIA+ rights, mental health awareness and support, fair pay for creatives, and productive self-care. In their downtime, they like to craft, cook, and dream up new projects. Their creative hub is melgcabral.com.

Rae Allison-Stork (they/them) is a 20-year-old genderfluid person currently attending a local community college in pursuit of a creative writing degree. They hope to be either a published author or a concept artist. Along with drawing and writing, they can be found fostering kittens. You can find more of their art at artisticrae.carbonmade.com or on their art blog artistic-fate.tumblr.com.

Ronan Sullivan (they/them) is a teenage nonbinary artist and author. You can find more of their art, particularly focused on digital drawings, on Instagram as @seal.does.art.and.stuff.

Shunamara "Mars" Trippel (they/them) loves to create all kinds of art. From drawing to writing poems, they try all kinds of things. Their favorite thing to do is cuddle with their kittens Simon and Topaz while making comics. More of their work can be found on instagram as @marsbarsdraws.

Sidereus (they/them & xe/xyr) is an animal lover with the occasional urge to make art. They're still coming to terms with their nonbinary identity, but they hope that one day we'll be able to embrace the full spectrum of human expression without judgement or persecution. You can find them on Tumblr as @khajiitofficial.

Theo Hendrie (he/him & they/them) is a blue-haired nonbinary YouTuber, writer, artist and poet. Their work focuses on raising awareness of and advocating for trans people and their channel covers everything from looking at current issues through a queer lens, to LGBTQ media recs to teaching the basics of trans identity to confused allies. You can find them anywhere on the internet as @genderpunksap.

Xanthe Wood (they/them) is an 18-year-old artist whose dream is to draw and create for a living. They are struggling to come out but in the meantime are living through their characters and stories. You can find them on Tumblr as @lonelyhorrortea and on Instagram as @golemofthewoods.

Glossary

AGAB - an acronym meaning 'assigned gender at birth' or, in other words, the gender the doctor believed you to be when you were born. The acronyms 'AFAB' and 'AMAB' mean 'assigned female at birth' and 'assigned male at birth' respectively.

Agender - having no gender or a feeling of genderlessness.

Cisgender/Cis - your gender/personal identity are the same as your assigned gender at birth e.g. if you were born and the doctor said "it's a girl!" and you still identify fully as a woman, then you're a cis woman.

Cisnormative - the assumption that all individuals are cisgender e.g. statements such as "If men could get pregnant" are cisnormative since trans men can get pregnant.

Exorsexism - discrimination against or erasure of nonbinary people.

Gender - an internal identity influenced by masculine, feminine and androgynous characteristics.

Gender dysphoria - the distress which may caused by the disconnect between one's assigned gender and one's true gender. Not all trans people experience gender dysphoria and those who do may experience it to a greater or lesser degree. Bodily dysphoria refers to the discomfort with body parts that are perceived as gendered whereas social dysphoria refers to the discomfort with being perceived as the wrong gender.

Gender euphoria - the joy associated with moments that are particularly affirming to your true gender. This ranges from having the correct pronouns used to wearing a suit/dress for the first time.

Genderfluid - having a gender identity which is fluid or fluctuates over time.

Gender incongruence - the disconnect between one's assigned gender and one's true gender.

Gender non-conforming - someone who does not present according to the stereotypes of their gender e.g. a tomboy or a man who wears makeup. This is not the same as being trans/nonbinary as the latter is identity/who you are (internal) and the former is your presentation (external).

Gender roles - the stereotypes and assumptions placed upon a gender or assumed gender e.g. girls like pink and boys like blue. These are largely socially constructed rather than innate as they have changed throughout history and in different cultures.

Genderqueer - someone whose experience of gender falls outside of purely masculine or purely feminine. This is a broad term encompassing a lot of different experiences. It is also a precursor to the term 'nonbinary' and originated from LGBTQ+ zines in the 1980s.

Intersex - a person whose biological sex is a combination of both male and female characteristics. This can range from ambiguous genitalia to hormone disorders to chromosomal variations (XXY, men with XX etc.). Intersex people are as common as redheads.

Misgendering - referring to a trans/nonbinary person as the wrong gender or using the wrong pronouns. This can be very hurtful and dehumanising as for many of us it happens often and erases who we really are.

Neopronouns - new pronouns invented to provide more gender-neutral options (as opposed to the gendered 'he/him' and 'she/her'). Some examples include 'ey/em,' 'xe/xer,' and 'ze/zir.'

Nonbinary - someone who is not fully a woman or fully a man. Nonbinary people can be a third gender entirely, have no gender at all, be a combination of genders or have fluid genders. Nonbinary is both an identity in itself and also an umbrella term for a huge number of other identities.

Non-cis - a term used to describe people whose gender is not the same as their assigned gender but who do not identify with the term trans.

Passing - the idea of presenting fully as your gender, so that someone cannot tell that you are trans. This is often not applicable to nonbinary people as most people will categorise us as either men or women no matter how we look.

Sex - a set of biological characteristics including your genitalia, reproductive organs, hormones and chromosomes. Typically sorted into 'male' and 'female' however this erases intersex people.

Transandrogynous - a term for trans people who are not aligned to either masculinity or femininity but neither or both.

Transfeminine - a term for AMAB trans people who are aligned with femininity. It is used to talk about the shared experiences of trans women and some AMAB nonbinary people.

Transgender/Trans - your gender/personal identity are different than your assigned gender at birth. Trans men were assigned female at birth but are men, trans women were assigned male at birth but are women. Many nonbinary people are transgender since our genders are also different than the one we were assigned.

Transition - a trans person changing their appearance in order to achieve their preferred gender presentation. Often broken down into social transition (coming out, changing name/pronouns, getting new clothes and a change of hairstyle) and physical transition (hormone replacement therapy and surgeries among other things).

Transmasculine - a term for AFAB trans people who are aligned with masculinity. It is used to talk about the shared experiences of trans men and some AFAB nonbinary people.

Acknowledgements

There are so many people to thank for helping this project to come to life and I am certain that I will forget at least one person who deserves to have a mention here - if that's you, then I'm so sorry. But know that I'm grateful all the same.

First, to my family for supporting this project and my coming out - it means more than I can say. And to my lovely mum, thank you for helping me to plan all this and come up with solutions to all the problems and for the hours spent networking during the crowdfunding and for a million other things. There aren't words to describe how much of your own work and time and effort went into this so thank you.

To Ben, thank you. For everything. Having you having my back for the last five years has been incredible and knowing that I could always crawl into bed with you after a long day has kept me going. I don't know if I'd have the courage to come out without you by my side so, from the bottom of my heart, thank you.

To my friends, thank you for putting up with me when I was on my phone at every single social event, and when I was working long hours editing. I don't deserve your patience, but I'm so glad you're all here to celebrate with me now.

And of course, a huge thank you to everyone on Twitter. To everyone who shared my tweets from the initial idea, to the call for submissions, to the crowdfunding links - it could not have happened without you all. This project went from an idea I had in my bedroom to a whole book full of art, and poetry and essays because you believed in it enough to think it was worth sharing. I'm so grateful. To Ash Hardell, Jeffrey

Marsh and Neil Gaiman in particular - you have been such icons to me so having you share this project meant the world.

Special thanks go to all the backers on Kickstarter who helped to make this project a reality. I hope you all know how much you've done for nonbinary folks by helping to make this happen, I hope you know how appreciated it is by not just me, but everyone who needed to see this book in the world. So from the bottom of my heart, thank you to Abelle Prince, Abs, Accolade Aula, Adam Benedict, Aeryn McCann, Aidan Shenkman, AJ, Alesia MacLeod, Alex Bramble-Rose, Alex Craig, Alexej Axis, Alex & Em, Alex Holmes, Alex Iantaffi, Alice Oseman, Alison Lam, Allyn E.H., Amadea Soltau, Amaryllis Quilliou, Ambrosia J. Webb, A.M. Sevin, Andrea Speed, Andy Harper Krouse, Angela Deschand, Angela France, Anna Harper Brownlee, Anna Loden, Anna S., Annika Kwast, Anxrali, Apollo Vídra, Ariadna Molinari, Ariel, Arne Jacobs, Artie Carden, Artie Firth, Artur Nowrot, Ashe, Atthis Arts, August Haver, Autumn G. Van Kirk, Autumn Wright, Barbara, Baron Von Papergreat, bbmd4, Bekah Caden, Ben Grimm, Bernardo Nara, Beth Friedman, Bex vanKoot, Blake, Blue Mahy, Bob Buechler & Mandy Rose Nichols, Bonnie G., Brian Dysart, Brian Hanechak, Brendan Schlagel, Brie Stevens-Hoare, Brigid Gaffikin, Brooke Haba, Brooke Wiegman, Brookie Judge, Brooks Moses, Brynn, Caeth, Cameron Lillie, Camilla Zhang, Cara Murray, Carolyn Barrett, C. Brennan, C. Daetwyler, Ceillie Simkiss, Chareth Cutestory, Charly E., Charlie Craddock, Charlotte Organ, Chelsea Sieg, Chris C. Cerami, Chris Weber, Ciar Moore-Saxton, Cin, Claire Dinn, Claire Nicholls, Clarke Doty, Clorinspats, C.O., Colin Davis, Coryl Addy, Dakota Lentini, Dani Higgins, Danny Jazzo, Dan "Praukse" Hunsaker, David E.

Bennett, David Nett, David S., Decker Library, Denny-Jo
Miller, Dev Singer, D. Franklin, Doe, Dwayne Farver,
Ealasaid, Echo, Edward, E. Hones, Elijah Awkerman,
Elizabeth Wynn, Ellie D., Elliot Draznin, Elliot Walsh,
Elsa Rose, Elya Arrasmith, Emery Nail, Emma
Lindhagen, E. Moorhouse, Eric K., Erin, Erin
Subramanian, Ether, Evan Clarke, Evan Ostroski, Evan
Windsor, Ezzy G. Languzzi, Faolan Read, Felix
Cattison, Ferris Fynboh, Fidel the Castro, Freddie,
Freyja K.A., Gemma Seltzer, George, Georgie
Bennington, Ginny Nawrocka, Hanif Abdurraqib,
Hannah Darby, Hannah Hixon, Hannah Ostpol, Haven,
Hayden McDaniel, H. Baxter, Hollie Satterfield, Holly
"Jamie" Jamerson, Holly Kybett Smith, Ilina, Isabel L.,
Ivy Krislov, J. , Jackie Guiseley Åman-Dahlin, Jack
Verhagen, Jaimi, JamC, Jamie Kramer, Jamie M., Jason
P. Burnham, Jaylee James, Jendi Reiter, Jen Hickman,
Jenn Rubenstein, Jess Butts, Jessie Oehrlein, J.
Kusluch, John Menninger, John & Solomon Costello,
Jonathan, Jo Newton, Jo Robson, JPL, Jules Robin Blu,
Julian Stuart, Julie Gorman, Juliet Kemp, Justin de
Vesine, jyte04, Kai Davison, Kali, Kara Leopard, Kate
Glanfield, Kate & Levi, Kat Feete, Katherine D'Ambra,
Katherine Hempel, Katie Lynch, Katie Wolseley-Charles,
Katnaipe, Kat Veldt, Kay, Kaycee Moore, Keefer, Kelly
Tweten, Kelsey Evan Rounds, Ken Finlayson, Keyo
Erin, Kieren Sz., KimFemetal, Kim MacDonald, Kit
McGuren, Kris Atienza, Kris & Runi, Kriss Levin, K.
Robinson, Ky Magdalene, Laser Malena-Webber, Laura
Clements, Laurel, L.B. Horne, Lee Colwill, Leisha
Hussien, Lenny, Lily "Blanche" Zen, Linsey Miller,
litEROTICon.net - h.EAR.t, L.M., Lois Stone, Lorrraine,
Lucy Fox, Lu "Ship" Everman, L. Zhu, Magepaw, Maize
Wallin, Malay G., Marcos Lanio, Marcy Brook, Marius
Thienenkamp, Mark Rachael Argent, Matt Hope,

Matthew J. Rogers, McKenzie Adrien Andrew, MeenahRay, Megha Baikadi, Melissa Jennings, Mer Weinhold, Micaela Godfrey, Michael Goins, Michael Moore, Michela, Michelle MacQuarrie, Mike Hector, Miles Holcomb, Miranda Aguilar, Mira Strengell, Mouka & Afiel, M.V. Ho, Naomi Norbez, Natalie, Nicky Tyler, Nik Clark, Niki & Benj, Nina Rose, Noam, Noël Chrisman, Nora Gause, Octavia Butler, Olivia Brown, Mx., Olivia Montoya, Oskar Zeino, Paige Kimble, Pauline Joseph, Paul Ryan, P.F. Anderson, Phil Adler, Phil Giles, Poul Kiely, Quinn Pollock, Rachel Jones, Rachel Tan, Rea Matchett, Red Lhota, Ren Grayson, Rhian Beam, Riane Torres, Richard Lewis, Rikki Dennis, Riley S., River Edwards, Rob N., Ronnie Ball, Rosie Yakob, Rowan Chavira, Rowan Pierce , Ryn Daniels, S.A. Crow, Sam Pascoe, Sarah Sammis, Sara Väätäjä, Sarge2401, Sasha Boig, S. Cappi, Sen Keen, Seren, Serenity Rockwood, Shea Marazita, Shoshana Kronfeld, Sidney Ross, Silver Adept, Skye, Skye S., Sophie Stewart, Stefan Dellmuth, Stephanie A. Fox, Stephanie Beach Magic, Summer Lander, Susan Gilbert, Susan Parrott, Syntia Treeman, Sysco792, Tabitha Stewart, Tanner Vogelgesang, Tara Searle, Tasha Turner, Taylor Hosford, Teresa Martin, Terry M., The BE Hive, The Conciliottoman Family (and their penguins), The Owens Family, Tifa Robles, Tim Campbell, Tim Vaughan, T.J. Dominguez, Todd Leber, Tom Newby, Tyler James McMaster, Tyler Marcoz, Tyler Smith, Valerie Warhol, Valour Horsley, Violet Figueroa, whatsideareyouon, W*lfr*d, Yuri, Zac Ebenstein, Zachary Groff, Zetetics, Zoe Berkana, Zoe Jones, Zoe Riddick, Zoe Wilde, Zvi LikesTV, 98AE73 and all of those who didn't give their names - we couldn't have done this without you.

And last but not least, thank you to all of the contributors - I hope you know how much your words and your art matter. I hope you know that you deserve this place in the anthology and the world. Thank you for helping me to express what being nonbinary can be and I wish all of you every kind of success.

Thank you,
Theo

Printed in Great Britain
by Amazon